CADENCE

This 2020 edition of *Cadence* is dedicated to the memory of Robert E. (Bob) Blenheim, the award-winning poet extraordinaire whose leadership has helped make the Florida State Poets Association a vibrant organization. He is dearly missed.

CADENCE

Florida State Poets Association
Anthology Thirty-Eight ■ 2020

Published by
the Florida State Poets Association
book Design by CHB Media

Editors
Gary Broughman
JC Kato
Elaine Person

ISBN: 9798551270638

Printed in the United States of America

www.floridastatepoetsassociation.org

Cover Photographs
Front cover:
Linda Eve Diamond, Reflective Perspectives

Back cover, from top:
Nancy Hauptle MacInnis, Daily Walk of Dreams;
Daniel Stone, Cedar Key, 2017

Acknowledgements

THIS THIRTY-EIGHTH ANNUAL EDITION of the Florida State Poets Association anthology is now the fourth to wear the name, *Cadence*. This year's volume of *Cadence* is published in a difficult time. *Cadence* is usually introduced as a highlight of FSPA's annual convention in October, but because of the pandemic the 2020 gathering was cancelled. Yet, the quality of the poetry in this latest volume speaks to the health of the word-based arts in Florida. While whirlwinds swirl in the culture, poets are keeping the creative spirit alive, and in so doing are proving that reconciliation remains possible if we will only think with the heart. This truth is more important now than ever.

Readers will notice the front cover has an impressionistic quality caused by the irregular surface of the water on which the scene is reflected. It seemed appropriate for these times in which life in general appears to be not quite in focus.

In addition to poems selected from the submissions of FSPA member poets, *Cadence* publishes winners from the association's statewide student poetry contests in categories from sixth through twelfth grade. We are always amazed by the quality of poetry written by the young poets of our state. Our gratitude goes to Carolynn Scully, who manages the contest for FSPA, and to all the teachers who encourage their students to write.

The book also includes winning selections in nineteen categories of FSPA's annual poetry awards contest, which is open to all poets, no matter where they practice their craft. This contest is managed by Mary Rogers-Grantham. Our thanks to Mary for another successful contest.

Finally, thanks to all the poets who submitted their work, to the chapter leaders who encourage their members, and to my co-editors, Elaine Person and JC Kato.

— Gary Broughman, Editor

The Poems

FSPA CHAPTERS AND THEIR POETS

FSPA CHANCELLORS

FSPA 2020 POETRY CONTEST WINNERS

STUDENT POETRY CONTEST WINNERS

Sonja Jean Craig, External Geometry

FSPA

CHAPTER POETS

LIVE POETS SOCIETY
OF DAYTONA BEACH

Robert E. Blenheim

The Night of the Old Iguana

You're run-down and weary, old lizard.
Behind you, sin and rebellion: an unbridled life.
From Starbuck to Hondo you have run whores & robbed banks.
And killin's. More than you can count.
Common mortal laws, not your style.
You have only heard, with rapturous passion,
Whispering dreams of tequila and glory.

But now, a scorpion being eaten by red ants,
You sit here in Agua Verde, on a saggy straw mattress
Holding a nearly-drained bottle of tequila.
An old son of a bitch
Left only to dregs of ground-up dreams
And wishes of being a child again.

Before you a young woman dries her glistening smooth skin,
Brushes her long black hair like wind caressing the
                    fertile prairie grass.
Your gaze from grizzled face is met by soft warm eyes
And a look that could calm the wildest stallion.
For the moment, a Madonna, this whore.

Squinting, you suck down the last golden drops from the bottle
                    and hold it before you.
As empty as your life.
But as you peer within it, muses begin to whisper.
You have drunk your last bottle.
You have had your last woman.
Now it's time for the other.
Time to play your string out to the end.

So you rise wearily, buckling your cartridge belt.
Then, breathing both woman and tequila,
You drop a few pesos on the table and stride to the door,
A bedraggled and wizened titan with six-guns, loaded,
And face your comrades.

Let's go you say, each word branding the air with hot iron.

It is time for an old lizard to transcend the sunset
For a butterfly morning.

    -- To Sam Peckinpah

      Winner, First Place: <u>Poetry Society of Texas Award</u>, NFSPS
National Contest, 2020.

Cherelyn Bush

Answers

Seems like none are right
There is no agreement
Could be incorrect
There are no facts
Unknown information
They are always waiting
For impossible clarification

Vicki Iorio

She stuffed

the insurance check in the front pocket of her tight jeans,
took the car that didn't melt, that was hot, but started.
She scooped up her daughter and her daughter's bunny —
charred on one side, black and pink.

The house is the burning end of a cigarette. She floors
the ignition, the night smells of fire. She does not believe
she will ever lose that smell, it has nested in her hair,
her nostrils, her sinus, even her daughter smells like fire.

The insurance check is a fire in her pocket.
She has never seen that much money in a check
made out to her. He is coming around tomorrow to reclaim
the check. She will shower after she puts one hundred miles

between her and her destruction. She will stop driving
when she quits smoking, dye her hair and her daughter's
pink like the bunny.

Llewellyn McKernan

Upstart Pencil

I scratch Walt's back.
I kiss Emily's thumb.
I take the poet laureate
on a two-year run.

I ponder graphite.
I count what's here.
I bury Sylvia's
three gold tears.

Things turn up
like hand-hewn oak.
A march of marks.
A finger stroke.

Things turned down
become a shadow,
going back and forth
over all that matters.

What burns up
I can't abide,
but from its ashes
rises all that's mine.

Ellen Nielsen

Doppler Effect

The faster it comes, the higher the pitch
of the screaming siren.
You forget the scientific explanation
as you pull over to the curb,
and fumble for license and registration.
As blue lights fill your rear-view mirror,
you wonder what it's about
this time.
You know you weren't speeding —
not in this neighborhood.
Is your tail light out?
Did you forget to put the new
sticker on your old license plate?
Were you playing your radio too
loud, tuned to rap instead of country?
Did you fail to signal a lane change,
like Sandra?
Do you look like someone who
could have committed a crime,
like Philando?
Are you just
the wrong shade of brown
at the wrong time
in the wrong town?
When the police car passes by
the shrill pitch drops
and you remember
why.

Ruth VonNieda

First Safari Night

Ngoro Ngoro a volcano rim
It really grows chilly when sunlight dims
So sipping coffee bringing warmth in
Helpful when its hard to breathe
To peek over the edge was such a tease
At eight thousand feet, the air was thin.
Hearing "Natures call" behind my tent
I gasped to meet a huge elephant
Raising his trunk, he let out his stream
Remaining silent such a shocking event
I was distressed, the elephant content!
Hard to breathe thin air affecting me
Guides rushed me to rover emergency
Off the mount they want to take me
To give you relief so to help breathe free.
"Oh no, I must stay, this is my destiny."
Tucked in the rover meant to protect me
A sudden thrump, screech, a hi-he-hee >
Through the window a black tongue eyeing me.
A flood of light struck a blinding pause
Drooling, red tongue, piercing eyes mean
Yellow furry thing out of a movie scene
Only a windshield to protect me from open jaws.
The guides with rifles all were armed
This dangerous creature must not be harmed
Silence! Guide nor creature made a sound
The cowering creature swung around
Jumped off, leaving me totally alarmed.
Now, how to calm down from this awful fright
Guides gave "thumbs up" things were alright
The heroes waved saying "have a good night."
It all ended when they turned off the light.

Bruce Woodworth

What the Nights Held

I remember the smell of the bowling alley lounge
where our parents used to take us,
my sister and me.
Stale cigarette smoke, the bottoms
of ashtrays in my mother's breath
and beer in the warm cans.
They went there for the mixed drinks,
for the straight shot of bourbon
and the same sad acquaintances.

On the other side, in the lane area where
my sister and I played,
the smell was sharper -- the disinfectant
sprayed into those used white shoes with
the numbered red toes.
It was an alien world filled with lights
and colors, smoke and noise.
The sharp crack of the balls striking the
pins, the thunderous scattering.
The arcade — skeeball and pinball
machines, flashing and ringing,
ding-ding-ding-ding! -- a wonderland
fit for a prince and a princess.

Sometimes we would watch the bowlers,
confident in their collared shirts
and their wrist braces, soft-bellied archers
aiming into the hard triangle of narrow
necks ringed with red bands.
One leg slid behind the other, arms
held high above their heads like
ballerinas, they posed,
majestic as matadors.

We hated to leave, honestly.
Home was doors slamming, hard words

20

the residue of alcohol-fueled mood swings.
Cold dinners, our parents retreating into
themselves.
Sometimes, our father leaving after she
fell asleep.
A long evening of waiting and listening
with the sounds of bowling pins
crashing in our heads.

MIAMI POETS

Patsy Asuncion

A Proper Parting

I'd expected my end
to be expected

a sign at the terminal
   definitive arrivals
   departures
set times for adieus
   complete sentences
   accurately punctuated.

I'd assumed close friends
at my sickbed

revelations, redemptions
   a chance for closure
decadent chocolate
snuck in by my best friend
   with her own fork.

I'd never thought
about what to say

before final breath
   accepting family as is
saying sorry
professing love
making peace

I wish I'd known
I would wait too long.

Cyndee Levy

Quarantine Existence

Life on hold, a pause to reflect,
recalibrate - who am I? Wounds
and beliefs sustained as sacred,

wrapped in fine fabrics for safe
keeping are up for re-examination.
The past serves no purpose for

forward energy. What I thought
was precious only collects dust and
weighs me down. During this alone-time,

I gently let whatever I hold tight
to float into the ethers, without force
or coercion, no begging or deal making,

no fond farewells. Walls come down, a
readiness to clear and heal, no resistance
to change remains. In allowing, heart and

mind, free from lifetimes of heaviness,
are open and light. I move on a path of
new normal. At my deepest levels, I dream

of experiences I desire and allow them
to find me. It is within this present moment
alignment, my life of meaning is found.

Connie Goodman-Milone

Little Owl

Little screech owl,
bright eyes beaming
on leafy palm branch.

Mockingbird and blue jay
come in to harass.

Knowing his power,
Little owl stays the course
and stirs not an ounce.

Pat Bonner Milone

Balmy Evening

Banana trees,
like tipsy lovers,
lean against each other,
leaves draping across
their ripening bunches

Gibbous moon glows
through gossamer clouds,
blushing pink behind the veils

Coconut rum
teases the tongue,
conjuring a Caribbean mirage
memories of islands,
we were so young

Rosa M. Douglass

Pareidolia

I see an alien in my fence
A woodpecker too and
A phoenix in flight
Leaving the scene

I see faces and
Oddly posed bodies
Of real or imagined
people and animals

I see them in
Clouds
Wooden fences
Wallpaper
Tree bark
Marble tiles
Rocks, leaves
Ceilings and
Pavement…

What do I see
When I look
In the mirror?

Tere Starr

Airborne

Braced for a troubled landing
strangers touching hands,
each locked in our silent thoughts
of memory and prayer.
Time itself slows and spirals
as if it's winding down.
I see a woman screaming
and yet I hear no sound.

We're floating over treetops
held up with angels' hands.
I'm afraid to close my eyes
as if my view is needed.
And then I see a runway
covered with white foam
with fire trucks and rescuers
welcoming us home.

We circle once as wheels descend.
I hold my breath when suddenly
we're gliding on the ground.
The runway ends.
The brakes take hold.
We cheer, embrace and cry,
so thankful that
what might have been
did not include goodbye.

Lori Swick

A Walk Through the Wood of Your Departure

The grays deepen as the path sinks into the
cedars —
    red bark stripped from the moist white wounds
    it was supposed to cover.

Topaz eye of the great horned owl
 rivets every borrowed step dared by any furtive
thing.
 I did not see it open,

But it is as easily sensed as the silent scream
    of the fat orange sun purpling —
    while the canyon walls scrape it to the entrails
and suck it down.

The winds of dusk are heard long before
    they shake the falling shadows, rush around my
shoulders,
    and fill my ears with mocking laugher.

My soul is the abandoned sparrow's nest
    weathered into the half-dead oak tree
    at the lowest turn of rock.

Giant acorns drop —
    pot-shots in triumphant dark
    — an occasional "plop".

An eerie knowing rattles the leaves left on that
tree.
    To walk beneath them is to eavesdrop
    on my own nightmare.

And the loneliness —
    the moon is but a pock-marked pearl
    in that black pool.

NEW RIVER POETS

Peggy Burgess

Morendo

The harp is still,
no fingers poised above its strings
to charm them into life, nor will
its shimmering music fill
our hearts again; it sings
no more.
The piano stands
forlorn in brooding reverie,
remembering the agile hands
that swept across its keys in strands
of soaring melody
before.
I find no solace here
in this familiar room,
no sweet release of healing tear;
its silence beats upon the ear
in ponderous chords of gloom.
I close the door.

*Note: morendo is a music dynamics term (such as
crescendo or diminuendo).
It indicates "to die away".*

John F. Foster

Beach Ballet

Basking in beach-towel sleep,
toes sand-snuggled,
she dreams of dolphins dancing
upon the water.

Her deep, regular breaths keep time
with the rhythmic lapping along the shore.

At the first touch-tingle of rising tide,
she becomes one of the dolphins,
toe-dancing the surf,
as beach umbrellas pirouette
to the flute-whistle of the wind.

An arabesque of swans glides in,
performing their tour en l'air,
feathers synchronized to dip and soar
above the glistening stage.

A dolphin-girl now, she takes her cue
in a fishtail glissade, cresting a smooth wave
which carries her gently back to....

a salty taste of terry cloth.

Beverly A. Joyce

All These Poems

Here I sit with my ink pen
Hoping words will come again.
Often poetry can be a fight.
Is there nothing new to write?
There's been poetry for love
Hymns to praise God above.
Anthems to declare national pride
To describe the countryside.
Ballads that retell history's stories
Of others' famous follies and glories.
Poems to observe the holidays
Poems written in so many ways.
Poems we have recited for years
Bringing us laughter and tears.
Poems that plead peace and mourn war,
Poems and poems and poems galore.
Poems are part of you and me.
What will our next poem be?

Andrea McBride

Baby's Giggle

Begins
as a tiny splash of drizzle
on the walk,
works up
to the prayed-for,
dancelike, world-rinsing
kind of rain.

Meg Roman

Twilight

Raindrops cling to glass reflecting light
from within as darkness steals in
covering all but the sounds of water
dripping and faint thunder rumbles,
rolling away in the distance.

black cat lost to dreams
night setting for symphony
cricket lullaby

Susan Stahr

The Hiding Place

What's that sound — does he hear me — I'd better stay here
I'll remain very quiet or it's my turn I fear
This door of the closet should hold back the sound
Making him think that I'm gone — not around

It's dark and it's quiet — perhaps I'll open the door
Peek out — and then run — oh he's coming once more
Now don't move a muscle — stay right where you are
And don't breathe too loud or the silence you'll mar

His footsteps grow louder — he's getting closer to me
If he passes - not stopping — I'll try to flee
Is he leaving — I can't tell — oh why am I here
What's going to happen my heart's pounding with fear!

What if he finds me and pulls open the door
Oh what did I pick this scant hiding place for
His footfalls approach heading right back this way
There's no time to run — so in this closet I'll stay

His footsteps they stop — the knob is turning I see
It's the end of the line — what will happen to me
The door is yanked open — I've no defense — here I sit
As he grabs on my shoulder — he shouts 'Tag you're it'!

Winner 'Editor's Choice Award' From:
The National Library of Poetry
Published: 'Between the Raindrops' Anthology, 1995

Dina Tanner

Thirty-Two Lines

She seems
so mean
to make
me work
this hard
as I
begin
the task.

Words clump
inside
my brain
like damp
brown leaves
I've swept
along
 the curb.

I think
it's tough
to write
with just
two sounds
per line
and make
some sense.

This verse,
the last,
has proved
to me
it can
be done …
and was
not fun.

Cheryl A. Van Beek

After the Storm

Sheltered in the bush,
he'd watched his story unravel.
Now wind weaves
through its torn strands.
White glow
stitches clouds on gray canvas.
He re-spins loose threads
that catch water and light
in the sticky spokes
of his cartwheel web.
Stretched tight
over a rain-sequined loom,
needlepoints of light
pierce beads
orange, violet, blue.

Janet Watson

Dog Days of Summer

The
shadows
lay heavy
and motionless--
no relief from heat,
when August baked each day.
Our dogs panted, tongues dangling.
Then distant thunder promised rain
that was suddenly, slashingly, here.
Our dogs tucked tails and hid beneath the porch.

Betty Ann Whitney

Sacred Silence

One thing is certain
        to grace shifting air
                in one fluid swing

through brighter sunshine
        narrow transparent
                net-veined wings

stretching
        emerging from leaf-broken-light
                her crisp and sparkling

slender body
        like a needle darning
                marvelous design —

the dragonfly
        flexible flowing delicately
                yet so alive

sailing-off upwardly
        sashaying smoothly fairylike
                over field green grasses

        and meadow flowers of every color . . .
        returning dipping
                crystal wings glistening

sinking earthbound lightness
        gracing the hunt
                for earth beauty.

NORTH FLORIDA POETRY HUB

Pat Krause

A New Perspective

Focusing on what is
while aware of what isn't
Grounded in prayer and poetry
Not always optimistic
as worldly woes loom large
But hope runs deeper
fed by springs of faith
So much suffering
weighs heavy on the soul
Living in the present moment
becomes a daily goal
So much of life is still on hold
and staying put is getting old
Dawn to dusk…
some days the hours crawl…
and clocks move not at all
Immersing myself in nature
brings a sense of peace
Thanksgiving then displaces fear
Gratitude drowns out the din
and calmness settles in

Ruth Van Alstine

The Rhythm And The Rhyme

Minutes pass,
slip to hours,
peering at the page.

empty thoughts,
clumsy words,
a non-effective phrase.

easy may seem,
at first glance,
the rhythm and the rhyme.

wrinkled brow,
darkened room,
poet grinds the lines.

Sally Wahl Constain

Perfect Timing

This evening on a random ride, we spy,
peaceful protestors holding up picket signs
along four corners on Racetrack Road.
We are not racing, but my heart
skips a few hopeful beats on this
quiet street.
Folks standing up, standing proud,
quiet, not loud.
Their placards promote
the true American claims to fame.
justice and fairness, kindness, and peace.
I am reminded of Gandhi
and Dr. Martin Luther King.
Leaning out the side window, I thank them with a wave.
They welcome me to join them.
I would if I could.
The aches and pains of advancing age hold me back.

But my spirit is young, and it soars
in union with their sacred pleas.

ORLANDO AREA POETS

Teresa TL Bruce

Coming Attractions

orange blossom intoxication
mulberry purple hail-stains
scarlet amaryllis trumpet explosion
oak pollen yellow fluff rains
rose-green tomato expectation
white-star jasmine's scented refrains
black-and-red love bugs' public copulation
transparent dandelion airplanes

Lela E. Buis

Find Me in a Morning

Find me in a morning.
I am a calm sky
And the first twitter of birdsong.

The song moves along
As the day warms and the shadows shift
As the earth's turning exposes us
To the sun's harsh, revealing light.
Revealing of flaws,
Reveling of lies,
Revealing of weaknesses
That pull us down slowly
Into the mire
Of self-destruction and hollow endings.
Revealing of strengths
That lift us into warm spaces
And the love of family and friends.
Revealing of realities
That form and flow around us
Like the changing light.

The light moves and shifts,
Easing toward sunset.
It darkens and pools
In green shades and shadows.

Look for me there.
Find me again
In the dusk of evening.

Chris Flocken

Bougainvillea Dreams

A wall of fuschia,
wafting in the breeze
backlit by a clear blue sky
pretty as you please.

Bougainvillea —
such a pretty sight
climbing stucco walls
to terra cotta heights.

Evoking happy memories
of San Diego trips
and Tucson patios
enjoying tortilla chips.

I grow them now in Florida
to feed my hungry soul.
They ease my longing heart,
but going home is my goal.

Alice R. Friedman

Heaven

I imagine your idea of Heaven
is the lake at night
the booming bullfrog's bass
bouncing off the mountains.

You're a child again climbing Cobble   then
you're a teenager atop the lifeguard tower where
    you run the world.

College.
You and Neal put a red light on the girl's dorm
while the proctor sleeps in his car.
    You two run the student Fire Department.
I bet you're together again
    watch out!

I imagine your idea of Heaven
is that first trip with Becca
    swaddled so tight, only her nose pokes out
            Or
dolphin diving with Emmy
family camping in the Everglades,
Passover in Forrest Hills.
    The children ask the four questions
    Papa drones the service
        And
    Grandma Sara chatters with her sisters.

I guess you and Papa are together again
I guess you are together again with
Grandma Sara and her sisters.

I imagine your heaven is family
and we'll all be together again
        someday.

Peter M. Gordon

A Cold Dish

Vengeance is mine, saith the lord.
Does He keep his list
on a dog-eared paper
inside His wallet, like I do?

Old names scrawled
in pencil now smeared.
Yet I remember each one
as if I wrote them yesterday.

Which in some cases,
I did.

Where are you now, David Friedman?

You measured your grades
against mine for six year at PS 197.
Said we'd check in 30 years later to compare
piles of money. You never showed.

Are you in jail, Douglas Novick?

Terror of my Brooklyn neighborhood.
Knocker of books out of hands.
I've worked out three times a week for 40 years.
I bet I can take you now.

Sam Hearn, who stole my high school girl

I hope you still live together out of spite
dreading your 39th anniversary.

My bosses who downsized me

I heard you were all fired by
new corporate sharks that ate the company.

You, out there, who cut me off
yesterday —

Tremble
before my verses.

Carl Johnson

The Swallow

In fluoroscopy, after a sip of barium,
he sees his little birdlike swallow
falter in flashes of an eye,
sip from lip to come-hither
tip of tongue —
the gulp erupts like a brick
tossed into a well of mumbles.

Down, down the throat
the cool metal sloshes
around the epiglottis.
Eddies in a small catch basin form.
Water, once friend, now interlopes
in this space of air,
drops down like hardness
to an unarmed pipe.

A cough of dried leaves
rises, spastic. He harkens
for that old voice, now hidden
under brushwoood
where a small song wren
once *sang,*
gone now,

in this choke of winter.

Ngan Ling Lung

Am I Forgotten?

MaMa, MaMa,
The sky turns dark.
Am I forgotten by the Sun?

No, my dear.
You are not forgotten.
The Sun is still here.

MaMa, MaMa,
The air turns cold.
Am I forgotten by the Sun?

No, my dear.
You are not forgotten.
The Sun is still here.

MaMa, MaMa,
The day turns into the night.
Am I forgotten by the Sun?

No, my dear.
You are not forgotten.
The Sun is still here.

My dearest child,
I will hold you tight.
We will sleep through the dark cold night.

At dawn,
The Sun will rise,
As promised.

Holly Mandelkern

Listening to Stephen Vincent Benét (1898-1943)

He made us laugh at presidents;
he made us cry for slaves.
Abridging lengthy lives for us,
how much time he saves.

He brandished men who crafted war
in the sting and solace of words,
patriots in counterpoint —
and those who fancied birds,

John Brown's body (he died too soon),
Abraham Lincoln's paces,
John James Audubon, Daniel Boone,
fire from Southern places.

We met them dressed in his smart rhyme
in ballads of famed and small,
Southern gents and frontier brave,
and how he knew them all.

His schemes transcended place and time
in rhymes we understood —
the faces of Americans
unveiled both bad and good.

In school his voice was read from books
but now I've heard his birdsong —
the warble in his narrative,
beauty in a diphthong,

a quarrel of sparrows perched in trees,
the peck and pick of crumbs.
He longs to be a sparrow taking,
taking life as it comes.

Their heartbeats rapid, flesh of heat,
every day a spring
happy from dusty tip to tail,
and only some sparrows sing.

His mind knew cardiology
and laughter of the birds.
What of the cry of his own heart
and how we loved his words?

Rick Mandriota

Summer's Heart

Her voice was crushing
ball-peen and hard,
blowing the air
with a quick summer's heart.
She ruled in August
her breath quite strong,
blinding my shadows
with sun-filled songs.
Speaking through words
all remained in fiction
of unjust understanding
and cold-hearted coalition,
engaging my heart
its will survive
in the heat ... of the summer.

Mary Marcelle

Puppet

Hike up your dungarees
Make up your time
Tie up your golden tresses
Weld up your mind

Random noises invade the surface
Random scenes from a play
Random access to the alter
Random endings of the day

Boots crunching across the pavement
Chips crunching out the noise
Tires crunching gravel spraying
Fists crunching fighting boys

Puppet master pulls the strings
Puppet players on the stage
Pretty puppets in the photos
Made my friends feel in rage

Porch sitting is for the old folks
Put the crazy ones on display
"We always put them on the front porch"
Was what my mama used to say

Race into the grocery store
Race your brother for the phone
Click your race on online forms
Learn to race a high-speed drone

Take your shoes off, put them on
Shoe a strong horse for a show
She's a dark horse, plain and fast
Her dark mane fires a shadowy glow

Take a respite from this exercise
I'm running out of words
Respite makes my mind nap wholly
Mini-sleep is for the birds

Wake the dog to have her supper
She's old and tends to stray
The dog's dementia make me shudder
She doesn't know who I am today

Work it girl, shout at the drag queen
Make it work on reality TV
Go to work is a suggestion
"Work," they said, "would make you free"

Take the path through giant redwoods
Stray from the path that you don't like
Make your own path through the desert
It's a path for an adventurous hike

Frank T Masi

Food Immigration

This is an American crisis
exceeding the march of Isis.
It's the scourge of the nation
worse than high taxation
or the cost of inflation.
It's the steady onslaught
of food immigration.

Countries far and wide
send armies of food
to capture our tastes
oftentimes targeting our waists.

English muffins or French toast
initiate their march early.
Columbian coffee and Canadian bacon
advance as we struggle to awaken.

Belgian waffles and Greek yogurt
stand at the ready
along with Danish pastry
for something even more tasty.

Food migrants hide in shopping carts
seeking late night forays.
Polish sausages and Swedish meatballs
slink to the bottom to avoid recalls.

Libation takes up the rear
as Scotch Whiskey and Irish Cream
or an aged Italian Red
quietly lulls us into bed.

But alas,
American defenses are no match
and cannot withstand the assault.

We can only offer:
American cheese
and Apple pie
and claim this is not our fault.

Diane Neff

The COVID Limerick Suite

Praise those who are in isolation.
For those who see no obligation
        for heeding the rules,
        in shops and in schools,
"Please mask during your congregation."

The distance assigned is six feet,
to safely go forth in the street.
        Yet many are crowding
        the stores they are scouting –
for TP, they're willing to cheat.

I wish I could choose hibernation
instead of this self-isolation.
        The virus – persistent,
        and yet we're insistent
that distance will grant us salvation.

The worries I carry unbidden,
in this time of COVID, forbidden
        to utter aloud,
        affecting the crowd
as if chaos could remain hidden.

Although this is not taken lightly,
sometimes we must smile and say brightly,
        I'm doing just fine,
        although that's a line
to ease our anxiety – slightly.

Elaine Person

Alexander Hamilton in Paterson, New Jersey

The first Secretary
of the US Treasury
knew our country needed
independent industry.
Alexander Hamilton
Hamilton in Paterson
Founder of the SUM:
Society for Establishing
Useful Manufactures.
Due to Hamilton's smart guess,
the city was a huge success.

Lafayette and Washington
picnicking with Hamilton
where they dined on ham and tongue
at the falls in Paterson.
Sitting on the grounds, and then
Hamilton looked around, said, "Men,
as I gaze upon these shores,
I think that the water's force
can become a power source
to create a stronger course
for industry." That came to be.

Not his place of origin–
his home was the Caribbean–
yet Hamilton breathed oxygen
into the brand-new SUM.

Due to how the water runs,
Paterson made Sam Colt's guns,
was the country's great Silk City
making fabric that was pretty,
manufactured submarines,
airplane parts, government machines.

62

Helped out by the Great Falls' froth,
the US Navy had sailcloth,
and steam locomotives for Civil War.
With hydropower, the city grew more.

Manufacturing started
thanks to Hamilton's creation.
This statesman is a part of
the history in our nation.

Lynn Schiffhorst

Memory

An unseen house
on an unseen ground
upheld by angels.

The angels go in
at its doors and windows
as pitchers dip into a well

and come out brimful
of whatever it is
I want to remember.
Without one sign
I ask the angels
for what I need

and without one sign
they are already
handing it over the threshold

for not even I
can set foot in there

Carolynn Scully

I Can't Breathe

when I watch a man struggle from
another's knee pressed hard
on his neck squeezing his
windpipe against the pavement

when I imagine the broken heart
of a shattered mom who watches
and hears the moment a circle
of merciless monsters ignite her loss

when I think of innocents in the path
of out of control mobs with demands
but mindless when they bruise and
crush those integrated with them

when counting the daily numbers
of those who can't breathe
in the battle against their bodies
and those who are lost in this war

when behind my mask I watch eyes
wanting to be named, touched,
and valued — like me — in community
where we all are free to breathe free

Juli Simon

Not Enough

Imagine my surprise when
the words slapped me, well and tidily placed
(for maximum impact):
"Kindness is not
Enough."

What was that, again?

Benign goodwill comes
easily to some — who lend a hand when needed
and stay late to clean up,
who have a smile for strangers
and send notes of
thanks.
Kindness, to those who practice it,
can be breezy as brownies taken to the sick;
it feels good to all concerned.
It has a life and intent and is hard to
malign, but, weighed upon the
scale of need, it lacks
Heft.

Possible that it becomes a habit; the light sweater
you take along, without a thought?
Armor is heavy and doesn't have pockets; so
I hold tight to my best intentions and hope we both
toughen up.
Well-meaning love on butterfly wings is
weightless as a whisper,
in a time of
Speaking Up.

Shelley Stocksdale

KITE FLIGHT

Chased by air streams,
        fed with wind dreams;
winging changing breezes,
dipping high and low teases
far from firmament, silken shrouds
dance with birds, skirt silver clouds.
Climb sky cotton ladder:
overcome time, space and matter
conquering pole and wire,
scaling palm trees higher and higher.
                Spirit resting on one, thin thread—
                moon pillow, star blanket, earth bed.

Emily Sujka

Privilege

I'm privileged,
To feel this rain on my face,
The umbrella braid tugs at my wrist as it swings,
My feet kick up puddles so the umbrella doesn't miss out on the rain.
The tarp on the nearby construction,
Obstructs the wind,
And hits the framework's body,
With crashes that hush,
No time at all,
For the wind to whip my hair,
Into face tattoos,
They're signs of life,
The imprinted pulse of my existence in the rain,
I'm privileged,
To choose
To feel the rain,
Enshroud my face,
With a coveted veil of wet hair,
My lace.

Jenni Sujka

Waves

A time we didn't argue and I follow your every thought.
It all started on that highlighter pink boogie board.
You calm as a cherry jam crepe on Sunday
Myself as reactive as my multicolored zoo hat.

It was simpler when you kept my mind ignorant
But as you can see, I was ready to roar.
Even at age 3 with the same waves behind me,
Were the same in front of you.

Stan K. Sujka

An Affair With A Rainbow
   (Art is an expression of love or it is nothing. Marc Chagall)

You spread the velvet red,
Heart flutters and flips
You feel a sudden burn for more
Veins swell of heat
Sweet trickle down your face, hand,
And thighs

 So you splash a little yellow and
Out of butter -lust
With the want of more!
Sun grows bolder
In its heat
Tickles toe tips and fingers —
Apply more paint!

Change the brush. Smear blue, white,
Turquoise, soft mysterious gray
Till the eyes fill with tears —
How can sea and sky flirt
With power, with passion?
The colors seem to lick the skin
Kiss the face, hands, chest, abdomen,
Dimples of Venus
As if too deep in the ocean or too close to heaven,
And you have a hard time breathing.

Grab a pallet knife of black
Making trees and branches to hold onto,
Close your eyes and
The absence of light haunts you
As if you had been long void of feeling.

This affair is turning to love,
Picture shapes, more strokes, more color
Hard strokes faster, faster and stronger
Till hands up thrown to the ecstatic air
The spentness of it all,
And you, done to this,
Pray a new fire.

Mark Andrew James Terry

Be The Distance

A social distance six-foot span
will thwart the virus bogeyman —
if we all stand with arms outstretched
just like the one da Vinci sketched —
and be the norm. It's not farfetched!

Coronavirus habitat,
a social distance six-foot span,
is breadth enough from frying pan
to safeguard arms of Marianne,
when bursts the burning bacon fat.

For one who is a hiking fan,
when cottonmouth lies in your path,
a social distance six-foot span
is near the length (you do the math)
to block that serpent's venomous wrath.

Banana spiders, orange and black,
their webbing forms a sneak attack,
when spinning webs the width they can,
a social distance six-foot span,
they set a trap for tasty snack.

We'll point to those who come too close
and make it clear that we oppose.
We'll ban them like a feuding clan!
Infectious is this safety plan —
a social-distance six-foot span.

Robyn Weinbaum

Memory Lane

Strolling through the halls
No.
Liar.
Racing past doors
tight corridors of madness
endless rows of closets
I pause
lean against one
hear the rustling, the waking.

What's behind that locked door?

My hand turns the knob
pulls, pulls cnough
so I can slide my eyes
past the doorjamb
still pressed safe against the wall.
The soft mewling shrieks to escape
to remind me
why I locked it up.

Cheryl Lynn West

Blue

Blue.
Her hair was blue.

Not blue black,
so dark that it
radiated shades of
mystic midnight with
moonlit shimmers.

Nor was it the blue white
of a snowy coiffure
atop the crown of
an elderly matron.
Hair teased into
a rigid sculpture,
tinges of blue
peeking through
sprayed curls
set for a week.

It was
simply blue.
A primary color in
the crayon box,
tip worn down,
wrapping peeled back.

A blue hue
spread across
the shell of
a dipped Easter egg,
dried, dull,
longing for a motif to
claim it festive.

She trudged past the
motel's front door,
reached the laundry room.
Fresh sheets stacked upon
the heavy pushcart.
Scrub brushes,
toilet paper,
trash bags to be filled.

She arrived tired,
left exhausted.
Nothing to cause
people to observe her
except
her hair was blue.

Shari Yudenfreund-Sujka

Corona Hope

While the world is plagued by the Corona
pandemic, birds build their nest outside my
kitchen window.
While people hoard toilet paper, the trees in my
yard leaf out and send their pollen forth.
And while people panic, the flowers of Spring
burst forth in brilliant colors in the longer warmer
days.
And while the world keeps spinning out of
control, the natural world shows us what hope
looks like.

OSCEOLA POETRY SOCIETY

Al Rocheleau

Of The Great Hofmann

I.

The Great Hofmann offered to his pupil:
Constance, Miss Keane, make a tempo and keep it,
       pin your rubato to it — you can stretch the rhythm
but not too far, as they all must follow,
and then you must come back to your time.

Always, always, play the spaces between the notes.

(And she used these advices her whole life.)

To Jorge, the Cuban Flash, he said:
       the descending arpeggio of your G Minor
is more difficult.
When you come down, lift the elbow
a little so the hand falls naturally.

(So The Flash used it forever, for every such demand.)

These were *little* things;
it is always little things that carry the power,
not large complexities; it is action, objects,
the stuff of which concepts,
who think so much of themselves,
actually are made, and actually are.

II.

He did not practice.
(He did when he was young yes, prodigy.)
He knew thousands of pieces from memory.
Shortish man, small hands!
His Op. 111 made more than

several virtuosos give up the piece,
because they knew he knew
what they did not,
what Beethoven knew.

III.

Horowitz had two pictures atop his Steinway.
Rachmaninoff. Hofmann.
The first, like a father revered, he had figured out.
The second, he couldn't.

IV.

He sipped the drink, which was brown
and iced. His third one.

I thought it was him, whom I'd seen
those years before. A student, me; a marvel, him,
in Carnegie Hall.
I finally had to ask
"Are you Josef Hofmann?"

      "I was."

I understood this, how we are always
who were were, after we are.
I am, too.

But I could never play like *him*.

POETRY FOR THE LOVE OF IT

Charles Hazelip

The Value of Critical Thinking

Something to keep in thoughtful minds,
curiosity leading to investigations
seeking who, what and why to find
how to achieve a true revelation.

Curiosity leading to investigations
depends on intellectual attitudes
of how to achieve a true revelation,
part of an investigator's aptitudes.

Depending on intellectual attitudes
critical thinking makes falsehood denied.
Part of an investigator's aptitudes,
assures the essence of truth will survive.

Critical thinking makes falsehood denied,
seeking who, what and why to find
assurance the essence of truth will survive.
Something to be kept in thoughtful minds.

Linda Whitefeather

Self Worth

She tries
Her very best
Every single day
But it is never good enough
To satisfy critics
Who live inside
Her head

SPACE COAST POETS

Janna Schledorn

Skinny-dipping at Lake Wauburg

Crisp linen skin,
skin before freckles and spots,
free of pink cherry moles
back then.

She dives into the still lake,
the lake where her children
will splash and learn to swim
free of sand sharks and stinging jelly fish.

The lake where her father
built a cabin in the absence
of intimacy after her birth,
lake back then where she swam
after dark, with a lover
in skin free

in skin free of time
in skin free of this place
free of blemish and wrinkle
in smooth darkness
in moonlight sheets
in her own skin

in some year in a lake

Anne-Marie Simonton

Cremation

Scorching tongues
lick the tree
tasting its mortality
searing the coarse skin
devouring brawny limbs
and twisted sinews
gnawing through
leafy fingers
chewing the carcass
down to stony embers
and pale ash
leaving remnants
of an incinerated feast.

SUNSHINE POETS

Angie M. Mayo

Morning Caller

Stop!
Barely dawn, each morning you come
    to my window to strike the glass
relentlessly and determined.
    It's like an artillery barrage!
Indeed, I fear I'm under attack
    not quite awake, no caffeine yet
you drive me to insanity.
    I can't fathom the reason
you peck, peck, peck.

Stop!
Such a little creature
    but what racket you make!
Your vivid red plumage
    a delight for the eyes
I'd welcome you to stay
    but your beak never rests.
My goodness, is it made of lead?
    It doesn't break, it doesn't stop
you peck, peck, peck.

Stop!
Why, I ask, such insistence
    to break into my room?
The vast sky is awaiting you
    beckoning to fly, to play.
But you prefer to come
    into my confined space?
There's nothing for you in here.
    Rather than heed my advice
you peck, peck, peck.

Stop!
Four walls imprison me

I would gladly trade places
with you — I'd soar over the trees
     letting the wind carry me
as far as the eye can see.
     Yet your sole desire seems
to get closer, much closer to me.
     To get my attention
you peck, peck, peck.

TOMOKA POETS

B.J. Alligood

Waiting for Snow

Why does he haunt me?
     Even now after all this time.

The echoes of his voice
     bounce off the walls
          to pierce my skin like acid arrows
     seeking the blood organ within.

A slow torture.

Memories, like leeches,
     come to suck me dry.
To leave naught but the
     crackly leaves of October
          to fall from my orbits.

I can only hope for snow
     and pray it will
          leave my thoughts blind.

Gary Broughman

A Scene Well Played

"I love you," he said, right on cue.
His delivery was pitch perfect, and
she took comfort in being on script.
Smiling, grateful for a line well said,
she threw her arms around his neck
and pulled herself close,
lips whetting lips.
After a moment he untied his tongue
and said again,
"I love you ... *so much.*"
The script seemed to beg for a
romantic pause long enough to absorb
such words — perhaps the silent exchange
of love-hungry gazes, but she pressed
her cheek to his and ad-libbed,
"Oh yeah, I love *that* ... so much, baby."

Neither of them needed much direction.

He was deep into it now, deep as
his talent could take him.
One could hardly know
if this was real life
or a scene well played.
Nothing existed beyond this moment,
for him, for her.
Can actors be taught to breathe
with such primitive passion?
"Only you baby,"
he growled in her ear,
"only you."
She smiled,
knowing he meant it,
knowing there was
just this, just now.
He, She,
love-washed
and needing
nothing more.

Niki Byram

I've Been Right Where You Are

Believe me when I
    Say to you, I've been
    Right where you are;
    I can totally relate.
Breathing that same air and
Feeling the depth of your despair.

I wish I could tell you
    Something to make it
    Easier to bear, be fair.
But truly, it's a journey one
Must chart on their own.

Only, please don't
    Do anything foolish,
    In the future you
    Will have your wishes.

In the meantime,
    Know that I'm
    Here for you and
    That I care for you.

Sonja Jean Craig

Luna's Mysterious Light

Luna lights up the night
with timeless stirring emotions
 She knows the mystery
 She feels your deepest
        Darkest
                secrets

Luminous satellite circles
in ebony outer space
Totally encompasses Earth
yet — she seems to be there
        for only
                you

Trust her with your open heart
insights ripple like ocean tides
Severs subconscious echoes
from the mind's prison
        Release
                Liberate

Moonlit wisdom holds court
on unsung songs of sensitivity
 Eclipsed passions long dormant
shimmer desires of dream treasures
        ignite
                Radiate

Mitzi J. Coats

Elvis the Turtle Has Left the Building

I heard the turtle before I saw it,
shaking, rattling, and rolling
around in a tin watering can
that lay sideways in the garden.
Stuck head first, its hard shell
jammed the mouth of the can
and it was unable to back out.
I snipped the metal lip into
furled petals against the edge
and lifted it out by its firm belly,
stubby legs flailing in air to escape.
I wondered how this primordial
reptile had survived millennia
against dangerous adversaries:
snakes and cliffs and drought,
but couldn't make its way out of
an immovable man-made obstacle.
Grounded on grass, it scuttled off,
Not looking back or with so much
as a thank-you, thank you very much.

Helen Cummins

Clouds of You

Clouds of you.
We see you
as we marvel at their shapes,
each cloud unique
but fleeting-
like you.
We feel you smiling down;
so blessed to have known you.
Our hearts ache.
But when we look up
we find solace –
knowing you live forever.

Marc Davidson

Rest in Peace

In my ambitious wand'ring o'er the world
I've looked for places for a footsore rest,
and resting ever when your flag is furled.
I've found a few, selected as the best.

Daytona's Boot Hill Cemetery's ground,
a small but lovely patch to place an urn.
A sandy hill, with trees and grass around,
where locals wait their turn for their return.

Pere Lachaise, the final resting place
for many famed who've ended their life's run,
is green and lovely, shows the world the face
of peaceful sleep when your great work is done.

Friedhof Wiesbaden Biebrich was quite nice,
with rows of lovely trees framing each walk.
And monuments you want to look at twice
and wish that those within them still could talk.

The Pyramid of Zoser rules the land --
around lies naught but desert, nothing grows.
Today we've weighted blankets at command.
He built a mountain to ensure repose.

St. Louis Cemetery Number Two
abounds with tombs that sit above the ground.
Survived the storm Katrina when it blew.
We wouldn't want the dead to be redrowned.

Dying, it seems, presents a world of choice,
as all will die as round the old world spins.
Just flip a coin and choose where you'll give voice
when heavenly choir practice time begins.

Colleen O'Leary

War of The World

We are all soldiers in this war
No branch of the service here
We are one, fighting for our
existence on this earth.

Losing battle after battle to this
enemy that cannot be seen.
Sucking life out the world
we once knew.

Engulfed with fear of another wave
Feeling helpless as our loved ones
succumb to this devasting
 virus.

Covid-19 has changed the way
people think, live, and realize
the most important thing in
life we had all along was each other.

A vaccine will save us from
this virus.
What will save us
"From Ourselves."

G. Kyra von Brokoph

One Word

words' inexhaustible strings
anger hatred sorrow
dread fear grief
hope lust love
braided together and bound

around the brain
like Saturn's rings
thoughts tangled in the strings
like caterpillars in a cat's cradle
race too rapid to form words

right words stuck in the barrel
wrong words burst like bullets
stop sudden like steps
on stairs in a stranger's house
holding their breath tension

filled with soundless words
that should not have been said
needed to be said
or said in a different way
or at a different time

suspended in terror
they tumble
through the pause
like wing crushed sparrows
sail through space

until one by one
they fall and fade unforgotten
for one like you
there is only one right word
and only at the right time

Mary-Ann Westbrook

Selenic Passage

The silent silvery moon
rose swiftly up the
soot colored horizon
slipped slowly across
the starry sky scattering
sparkling diamonds over
the saltant sea then slid
sleepily away from
the sneaking sunrise and
set with a satisfied sigh

Robert Stanhope, Around the Bend

FSPA

MEMBERS AT LARGE

Suzanne S. Austin-Hill

School's in at the Library

I thought the librarian was in charge of this.
It seems as if I've asked amiss.
She's not a librarian. They maintain the branch.
The volume of their work, an avalanche.

If not that, what might she do?
Please fill me in; I have no clue.
Outreach, reference, circulation,
technology, inventory, and education.

I date myself as I recall,
   when *one* librarian did it all.
Seen, rarely unseen, with so much to do;
   a very present help in knowledge pursuit.

She stamped your book out
   and without any doubt,
   was there once again
   when you brought it back in.

Today *the* Librarian must surely be glad,
   that included in the online ad
   is a staff of Guides, Associates, and Assistants, too.
Don't call you Librarian 'cause that's not what you do.

And among the most interesting changes I see,
   is that *the* Librarian can now be a he.

Pat Bastendorf

Home Alone (two, three, four)

Grandma---suckin' on a ring pop
            doin' the be-bop
            caught in a net.
                        (two, three, four)

Dad still---down at the detox
            fill up the juke box
            I'll just forget, (rest)
                        I'll just forget. (rest)

Sister---puttin' on her church hat
            datin' a wharf-rat
            can't stick to tea.
                        (two, three, four)

Buddy---stays in his own room
            he's gonna fly soon
                        don't bother me, (rest)
                        don't bother me. (rest)

Me-------having a birthday
            goin' my own way
            turnin' sixteen.
                        (two, three, four)

Teacher---tells me to get help
            I'm not a young whelp
            leaving the scene, (rest)
                        leaving the scene. (rest)

Hanh Chau

A Mama's Word

Do you know that a mama's word is always right?
                    Whenever it is asking for the truth
Despite that we don't want to hear
                    With a seeking own advice
For nothing is too silly
                    From the bottom of theheart
With a genuine promise
                    Of wisdom and guidance
Never think of her otherwise
                    And place any doubt on her
Because she will never portray
                    With any sign of lies and betrayal
even from the bad and good time
                    A mama's word is filled with profound
To share with honest and sincere
                    Like many lessons that were learned
In a lifetime memory not to be forgotten
                    Only with a sense of gratitude
A mama's word is a testimony
                    Embrace from all walk of life
For the protection of love and care
                    From thick to thin
That never mislead
                    A mama's word is always right
with it's own instinct
                    to never second guess

                Because she knows better than all
                    Do you all agree?

Christine Cock

Beginner's Mind, Again

Wading through pasture grass after dew's drenching
      Each step   a spray of fractured glass

Standing in verticle allegiance with a pine,
      stretching, always stretching —

because its trunk is scoliotic, holding
      compressed weight   as my own spine crooks.

I watch woodpecker, waxwing
      attending umbrels of elderberry, like seeded
chandeliers

until, a bit drunk, drop to the ground to get their bearings
      Grounded   but not placeless

and since they are not, neither am I
      which is a daily relief

Tree line open field sunlight on golden stalks leaves shivering
      never seen before   every day.

Linda Eve Diamond

Robin Rounds

rounds of robins sing in the spring
bobbins of robins merry on berries
blush of a thrush tipsy on cherries
with honeysuckle wine from the vine

bobbins of robins merry on berries
blush of a thrush tipsy on cherries
with honeysuckle wine from the vine
rounds of robins sing in the spring

blush of a thrush tipsy on cherries
with honeysuckle wine from the vine
rounds of robins sing in the spring
bobbins of robins merry on berries

with honeysuckle wine from the vine
rounds of robins sing in the spring
bobbins of robins merry on berries
blush of a thrush tipsy on cherries

rounds of bobbins sing in the spring
bobbins of robins tipsy on berries
thrush of a blush merry on cherries
with honeysuckle vine from the wine

merry bobbins of robins tipsy on
rounds of cherry berry blush wine
singing in the honeysuckle spring
rounding the divine sweet vines …

Melody Dean Dimick

At the Daytona Beach Veterans Museum

Son, Dad and I visited a war museum last night.
Stuck way in a corner was a small round table.
Draped over the table, a linen cloth, pure white.
Like a newborn calf, I couldn't keep my legs stable.

Bottled-up pain returned in the soft light,
for an empty chair retold the price you paid
when your helicopter vanished from sight mid-flight.
The missing man table honors the sacrifice you made.

Missing — a frozen mountain hid your crash site.
You answered our nation's call and gave your best.
As we stared at a candle symbolic of your bright light,
a vase with a single red rose put my heart to a test.

Curator said a slice of lemon on a white plate signifies
your fate was bitter one weather-doomed night.
We knew you didn't evaporate into smoky skies,
but your aircraft vanished from radar sight.

Contact lost, forcing us to wait for news of your fate.
Far too many sleepless nights I shed silent tears.
Dad and I waited — waited for word of your fate.
Salt sprinkled on a museum plate symbolizes tears.

Son, in your empty chair at the table, no other will sit.
An inverted wineglass indicates you cannot toast.
Experts identified you, using my DNA, and I lost it.
Though you'd downplay it, of your bravery we boast.

When we got home last night — your room as you left it.
Trophies you won beneath your poster of Earnhardt.
Near your bed, the desk you and Dad crafted.
For Dad and me to lead a normal life, way too hard.

Dads and moms know war's not a sport or game.
Soldiers don't always come back to play ball.
And survivors, saddled with guilt—aren't the same.
Heads hang fog low when brave soldiers fall.

A visit to a war museum made my knees unstable
I realized I'd never again hug you or smell your scent.
Couldn't blink back tears at the missing man table.
Bent my head until my salty tears were spent.

Tracy Duffy

Decaf

When the fresh scent of greenery
overtakes the fumes of commute
The cool air licks up the dew
wafting across my senses like petal nectar,
leaping across the dusty route sweetening the grime
Then, it is glorious morning aroma blend

Joe Dunn

Bridge Walk

The Intracoastal bridge ascends a view
That might be coveted by a buzzing plane:
Islands underlined by road and railings,
An artificial vista lacking vision.
(Instead I picture a little fictional peak
With all the open innocence of the sky.)

Early lights are floating on the first of dusk;
A sailboat motors tightly furled as if
Propelled by expectation through the silent
Water. I wish the snap and flutter of the luff
Had brought me to the center of the bridge
Where I had walked above the passing mast.

Too many intersecting wishes make me
Seek the comfort of the evening's padded air.

Nina Heiser

crossing the bridge

tangle me in the branches of your wild heart
let us like the first leaf from the rock maple fall
into a love as simple and strong as a promise

we'll bathe in copper patches of the mountain brook
after the unsparing rains of summer
deep in the woods where warblers call

to evening setting the skies a-flame
clouds burst open to fractious saturation
we'll bow in reverence to the intangible

Jill Jennings

Settling

I've got a hand-me-down life
in my thrift store clearance dress.
The color may be pretty,
but the fit is not the best.

In someone else's kitchen
with a dead man's frying pan,
I'm cooking up the future,
but my pancakes taste like sand.

I want something authentic
not four plain white walls,
where some past stranger's writing
is still waiting to be scrawled.

Dr. Emory D. Jones

Bad Rap

An apple fell from
The apple tree
And rapped
Sir Isaac Newton
On the noggin.
It was a eureka moment.

But in the beginning
Tradition says
It was an apple
That Eve gave
To Adam--

I say it was
Passion Fruit!

Judith Krum

How Much?

A claw foot tub and hand-embroidered guest towels.
I had to stop at the yard sale.
My fanny pack was slung around my waist.
Filled with single dollar bills and assorted change.
I strolled around the yard in my comfortable sneakers.
Piles of desperation were set out in neat categories.
Clothes hung from a horizontal ladder.
Plastic flowers in chipped vases
Counterfeited table centerpieces.
Matchbox cars, a Chatty Cathy,
An Evel Knievel Stunt Cycle,
Set out for kids to try.
Small kitchen appliances were plugged in for shoppers
To verify that the blender blended and the mixer mixed.
A box of greeting cards, all occasion –
Birthday, anniversary, get well, condolences.
Another table was strewn with rusty saws and hammers.
Magnets of Maine lighthouses and Florida beaches
Spread out across a map of the U S
Like tableware on one end of banquet table.
On the other end, an array of Glen Campbell CDs,
Still in their clear plastic jewel cases,
Sparkled like rhinestones on a cowboy jacket.
Faded pamphlets for trips to Galveston and Phoenix
Held together with blue rubber bands
Were piled like paper fences on the edge of the map.
The gray-haired and sunglassed proprietor,
Wearing loose Capri pants and a pink tee shirt,
Sat at a card table with her cash box.
I approached her.
"How much for my fistful of CDs?"
"$4.50," she said wistfully.
"You never listened to these?" I asked.
"No," she sighed.
"He took the CD player when he left."

Jim Loveland

[There Was a Little Girl Crying in the Castle]

There was a little girl crying in the castle,
For she found the long lines a big hassle.
  But her father was more concerned
  This place took all his money he earned
Just to see an overgrown mouse razzle dazzle.

NoirJente

No Wish

I have no wish to star
upon a thin cold stage,
reciting mundane vanity
to assuage the insecure.

I have no wish to spar
against a thin veiled rage,
contending with insanity
to persuade those less than sure.

I have no wish to fill
an empty cup of despair;
the failing is in narrowed sights,
not in any trespass made.

I have no wish to still
the cries of the unaware;
if you cannot stand the sunlight,
then, by all means, seek the shade.

Virginia Nygard

Flashes Before Her Eyes

Iris blooms beside the door
where my hero swept me up, and
in breakwater arms fended off the tides of life
that crashed and ebbed from time to time. But look!
These hands, these legs, all skin and spindly bones
with threads of blue streaking through...whose...?
Oh. Mine.

A nasty gift of cursed Father Time.
Father? Is it really you? Yes!
How I love your eyes like blue crystal,
your curly hair that tells the Black Irish secret.
You lift me up upon your lap and hug me
as if I were your only child, not one of ten.
Look! See?

The boys have all grown up to men
some with children of their own.
Some went to war and died. Some lived
and now in St. Michael's lie with wives and kin.
We last three, my twin, my little sister, me...
gone now, all but one. Who?
Yes. Me.

I am the missing face afloat the way
a Dali shape escapes the eye
in his busiest canvas scenes.
I'm a tiny dot the Great Artist has yet to place,
but since I am the last of ten,
soon I'll fill my spot.
Who? Me?

I'm number nine — but number one
with — who? Yes, yes, my daughter dear.
She keeps my house in perfect order,
dusts and fusses, and sweeps the rugs,

cooks and cleans, makes the silver gleam ...
So, I'll just bide my time until I'm called.
What? Now?

It's time to leave my home with—you?
The light's so bright! Please hold my hand?

Dennis Rhodes

Ride

for E.D.

I went for a ride with the earth.
It's such a silly sphere —
We traveled 25 thousand miles
yet ended up still Here.
I should have felt euphoria.
I should have felt a thrill —
to journey such a distance
by merely standing still!
I shall do it again today,
Pin my eyes to a star
and ponder how remarkable
the earth and heavens are.

Michele Parker Randall

Mocking
Bird

Purtypurtypurtypurty.
             Across the street, over the yard,
through closed windows, and under my pillow, flows
its raucous caw, which pecks behind my eyes and scrapes
the inside of my skull. My neighbor hears it closer, louder.
From the camphor tree outside her bedroom window, the bird
runs its repertoire of chirps, chits, and occasional clank deep
in the night, assisted by a spotlight moon.

Purtypurtypurtypurty.
             How does one deviling bird in predawn
gloom become the one thing we think we can change? She drags
outside a plastic blue bin filled with her children's toys and shoes;
one by one she chucks them into the branches, pitching until
the bin lays empty, yelling back at every tweet and twitter. *Purtypurtypurtypurty.* Her aim is off and her arm tires long before
the mocking bird's play-list pays out, and we all sleep a few
hours.

Rosa C. Rodriguez

Autumn

Summer closed its green door
To show up the reddish crossbreed
Of the expected Autumn.
The skilled paintbrush
That draws the new season
Designed by sunset,
Is tracing the path of the birds.
Nights are unique,
Their breath is full of dreams,
When the green foliage looks asleep.
I want to be part of the warm sun
That caresses the cold air
In the mornings of Autumn.
I want to embody the nude nature
And feel that I am
The diversity of color of the season,
The nostalgic romance of its days
And the silent fire that warms
The preamble of Winter.

Mary Rogers-Grantham

An Argument in Rhythm

I hear winds sweeping the sky
into a fury of storm clouds,
and listen as it walks
up and down the steps
like the rhythm of relentless
lightening chords.

I watch dusk running sideways
while playing hide and seek
with beacons of bouncing behavior
and barbaric rain,
like an argument
that refuses to end.

Darkness creeps in honeylike, and
covers evening with the blanket of night.

Evelyn Ann Romano

Crossing Over

Across the road, a white PODS square
like a giant icebox
roots in the driveway. A metal ramp
scrapes the concrete. The new neighbors
the third to buy this house
at seven zero seven White Wing Place
unload their belongings.

After many years I don't recall the people
who first bought there. I remember fledgling
oaks planted too close to unruly
magnolias and sturdy sod squares
nestled in rows. At the villa's entry
a small Bird of Paradise poked its orange beak.

Most residents are retirees. On White Wing Place
a smiling sun blazes: holiday galas, poker games,
block parties, bunko weave a fabric
and community unfolds. Neighbors become family
a forever gift.

Over time, the dark face of loss looks our way.
Ambulances rush in the night.
Street lights stutter and sound is noise. Sidewalks crack
and shrubs beg to die.

We try to cross the road and the setting sun rages.

* Published online in OLLI CONNECTS USF in April 2020.

Daniel L. Stone

Beauty of Life

Today gives the beauty of life
tomorrow may offer the same
or perhaps never come.

Standing here I feel the warmth of early sunlight
I hear the sounds of morning being born.
In the distance there is a shrimp boat trolling.

Tourists, some comatose are laid-out in beach condos
soon to bring offerings of stale bread and left over pizza.
 Hovering sea gulls are already squawking for the handouts.

My bare feet feel the soft sand.
I am surrounded by peaceful sounds of life.
The incoming tide gives a serene background.

If I stand long enough in the cold salty tide
it will soon wash over my feet up to my ankles
a feeling like slowly sinking into quick sand.

Closing my eyes the experience is enchanting.
Here breathing in the fresh ocean air I feel alive.
At this moment I am complete.

Today gives the beauty of life.

Daniel R. Tardona

Jivy Day

'Tis a jivy day

rollin' and rockin'
jestin' and jigglin'
enjoyin' and greetin'

while I was strollin'
along my way,

sunnin' and bummin'
joggin' and a jugglin'
dodgin' and gleamin

wow! I was thinkin'
what lively way to play,

hummin' and funnin'
jamminin' and a jazzin'
enrichin' and grinnin'

what more can I
say!

jawin' all that jive
just jolts
my noggin for a
jivy kind of day

Christine Valentine

All The Music

Give me music every day
A Sousa March in July
Beethoven blaring as the rain
Runs down the window pane
Tony Bennett while I iron
Symphonies with afternoon tea
James Galway in a summer lea
Slow jazz on a boat
With Satchmo's riveting high note
Mozart's Requiem in the deep forest
The Hallelujah Chorus at Christmas
And when I'm lifeless
A temperance band
So when they shovel in the sand
All the notes and rhythm
Will beat my heart into heaven

Lucy Venable

Valenmine

A photo captured me
before I was a wife
a mother

A moment between
the wave
forming

A moment where the breath
is neither in
or out

A pause
between the uncorking of the champagne
and the explosion

It was when
I was still
mine

Frank Yanni

Shooting Star

When young, we rode a shooting star
and toured the endless galaxy
got a peek at Heaven's gate
and heard celestial choirs sing.

Now, old age prohibits riding stars
and Heaven seems like some vague dream.
And yet, and yet, does
my heart faintly hear
celestial choirs...
            singing for me?

Helen Cummins, Sarasota Banyon Tree

FLORIDA STATE POETS ASSOCIATION

CHANCELLORS

Lola Haskins

Across the Tops

our path runs narrow through heather whose purple sprigs, being September's, are mixed with brown. A bleak sacramental wind cleans us for Rhylstone Cross and the miles that may remain to us under this dark-gray roiling sky whose blue patches open and close in a blink.   May no step we take go unnoticed, may we mark the whirr and complaint of each flushed grouse, and may we glory in the cold forever, for it is the cold of the sea, which is grass and heather and birds and sky, and most of all the breaking light that gleams, wild and holy, in our eyes.

From *Asylum: Improvisations on John Clare,*
(University of Pittsburgh Press, 2019).

Carol Frost

Labyrinthine City

An eagle chased the falling
in case the creature drop a feast of sinew and pulverable bone.

Blue-golden surface rushing up,
no branches breaking with honey petals

to soften the blow. No more cunning this day,

this world Icarian.
                          For the moment everything
stopped caring and those that could flew on.

                          ~~

A partridge laughed, secretive in his ground bower,
as the father fathered the drowned arms and head.

Were not other boys cast from heights,
made birds?

                          Horned crab, ant, and the mole soon
dig through the hillock covered with flowers.

Rain ravel in the dry loam. To walk there
would be to sense loftiness brought under.

                          ~~~

I saw your labyrinth as I rose, my head in spirals.
How could man trick from stone a river's running waves
flowing back to a blind source, then toward open sea?
Once started, how could there be a way back?
Winds roared as I flew, like the roar in my veins.
I breasted upward with the glittering rocking honeyed
air, my lonely impulse for ascent come from you.

I soared. And you must have felt – beyond your
fright for me - the splendor above – an open dome
you may as well yourself have flown to
with your own instrument of wood, wax, and feather.
Then as it came apart I was the ideal
falcon, earth the falconer spiraled to. Or I was an ant
in a triton shell tied to a linen thread
following sweet vapor in the chambers
to its source. The mind perpetually meanders
till eyes are shut, nothing, I thought,
bringing back or revivifying. Yet here we still are –
art and invention riding a fabled wing span,
out of nature, human in failure, telling of
son tied to father, father to son, telling of what is past,
the riddles we come from, and those to come.

From *Alias City* (MadHat Press, 2020).

Peter Meinke
Florida Poet Laureate

The Last Daiquiri

for K.K.

We watched the bartender stem and chop
the strawberries hands flashing in sunlight
knifing through the window   Our small shop
swelled with its ripe intoxication

of berries limes and pale white rum
clacking with ice cubes in the cracked blender
You hadn't been feeling well at all   some
twinges in the ticker tenderness

in the chest   But *This is the best drink I ever had*
you told us slow eyes sliding toward a joke
If I'm stuck before a firing squad
that's my last request – the hell with the smoke!

Well the bartender said giving another shake
Good idea   It takes some time to make

Denise Duhamel

Dear Memory

What have you done with my keys? I blame you
though it's hard to hold a grudge these days
because I usually don't remember
why I was angry in the first place.
I look at a person sure she's done me wrong
though the inciting incidents are lost. Former students
seem familiar, but their names disperse like cigarette smoke
blowing towards a stool where I once drank myself sick.
Now I'm not even sure what city that bar was in,
the welcoming pink neon letters, another cloud,
as though I am looking at tiny print
without my reading glasses. I was on a pink cloud
when I first stopped drinking. In fact, I once looked up
at the moon, weeping in gratitude. So there,
I do recall something! I was walking across
the Brooklyn Bridge in an ex's sweatpants
though I'm not sure anymore of his name or if I ever
gave those sweatpants back. I'm usually halfway through
a movie on Netflix when I realize I've already seen it,
probably in an old-fashioned freestanding theater,
perhaps a matinee or a midnight screening.
Perhaps a popcorn bucket on my lap —
that is, if I wasn't on some fad diet.
Did I take my pain pill or not? I'm drinking water
but not sure I can detect that bad taste all the way
back on my tongue. Maybe I have been drinking
more water than I thought. Is it time to go
to the gynecologist again? The office usually sends me
a reminder postcard, but today I'm holding
a letter from the Breast Center saying it's time again
for my mammogram. I usually get a prescription
from the gynecologist about a month beforehand — this is how
it's been the last few years. I wonder if my doctor is retired
or dead. I would call him, but I have forgotten his name.

It begins with an S and I think I remember the exit.
I look through the stack of business cards
I save for moments such as this, but no card for him.
I go to take out the recycling just moments
after I took out the recycling. I stand at the fridge,
its door ajar—the cold lightbulb, an idea for a poem
which I've also forgotten, a sublime dream
that woke me in the middle of the night, a sublime dream
I was sure I'd never forget. Ah, here is my key ring!
But this gold one with the big square head—
what lock could it possibly open?

From *Second Story* (University of Pittsburgh Press, 2021).

Virgil Suárez

The Cotton Ball Queen

In 1970, Havana, Cuba, my mother
took it upon herself to inject

B12 on the butt cheeks of as many
neighbors as brought her doses

and paid for her service. My mother
wanted to be a nurse but was not

a nurse, but the house filled with women
waiting for their shots and I, at eight,

watched them lower one side of their
pants or shorts or pull up a dress

to expose their flesh to the needle.
The needle disappeared into the flesh.

My mother swabbed their skin
with a cotton ball drenched in alcohol

after each shot and threw it in a bucket
by the kitchen door. When she was

not looking I reached for a handful
and went outside to look at how

the blood darkened. I wrapped my
toy soldiers in the used cotton.

They were wounded. Cuba
was sending military personnel

to Viet Nam. My mother shot up
more people, "patients," as she called

them. When my father came home
there was no trace of anyone ever

been over. My mother expected
me to keep her secrets. On the mud

fort I had built in the patio all my
soldiers lay wounded, bloodied

and dying.   At night I dreamt
of the house filling with mother's

pillow cases full of cotton balls.
In the United States, my mother

worked in a factory, sewing zippers
at 10 cents a piece. 25 years.

She never looked up from her machine.
Her fingers became arthritic . . .

Every time I cut myself shaving, I reach
for a cotton ball to soak up the blood.

Blood is a cardinal taking flight
against the darkening of the sky.

David Kirby

Taking it Home to Jerome

In Baton Rouge, there was a DJ on the soul station who was
always urging his listeners to "take it on home to Jerome."

No one knew who Jerome was. And nobody cared. So it
didn't matter. I was, what, ten, twelve? I didn't have anything

to take home to anyone. Parents and teachers told us that all
we needed to do in this world were three things: be happy,

do good, and find work that fulfills you. But I also wanted
to learn that trick where you grab your left ankle in your

right hand and then jump through with your other leg.
Everything else was to come, everything about love:

the sadness of it, knowing it can't last, that all lives must end,
all hearts are broken. Sometimes when I'm writing a poem,

I feel as though I'm operating that crusher that turns
a full-size car into a metal cube the size of a suitcase.

At other times, I'm just a secretary: the world has so much
to say, and I'm writing it down. This great tenderness.

From *The New York Times Sunday Magazine*,
February 14, 2016.

Silvia Curbelo

A Short History of Goodbye

The grass tells nothing.
The sky sits in its simple
cage of days. No sound
like the past blowing through.

Only the wind knows what's
at stake here, moving into
the scenery, running at the mouth.
Hush, say the daylilies

shaking their heads a bit.
Silence is its own music,
soft as dirt. No one notices
the orphan drift of clouds,

the wingtip scar of the horizon
balanced between nowhere
and this. *Hush*,
whisper the azaleas.

But nothing's as wordless
as a young girl standing on the lawn
waving her handkerchief.

From *Ambush*, (Main Street Rag, 2004).

Lee Bennett Hopkins (1938-2019)
Children's Poet and Anthologist

**Good Books,
Good Times!**

Good books.
Good times.
Good stories.
Good rhymes.

Good beginnings.
Good ends.
Good people.
Good friends.

Good fiction.
Good facts.
Good adventures.
Good acts.

Good stories.
Good rhymes.
Good books.
Good times.

Rosa M. Douglass, Lakeshore Heron

FLORIDA STATE
POETS ASSOCIATION

ANNUAL CONTEST WINNERS

CATEGORY 1 FREE VERSE AWARD

B.J. ALLIGOOD
Port Orange, Florida

My Mother's Purse

For me, in my thirties, it was not the treasured, expensive, seldom used items of
importance that triggered my grief after my mother's death. It was the common
every day items that, like a sneaky vine, would quietly loop about my ankles and
quickly jerk me off my feet, so that the pain of her passing would smack me
squarely in the face and knock the breath out of me.

Removing the small amount of cash and coins from her purse I felt like a petty
thief stealing from my mother while her back was turned. Just the act of sifting
through such personal belongings felt like a violation.

I found a "To-Do" list that was yet unfmished and in the act of crumpling it and
throwing it away I felt like the grim reaper cutting short an unfinished life. Never
would these chores get done.

Her driver's license, insurance card and credit cards all had to be cut up and
destroyed. But when I sat there, with the open scissors in hand, I couldn't bring
myself to make the first snip. It felt like I would be excising her arm so that her
hand would be unable to make the oh-so familiar swipe of a purchase and I feared
the frrst slice would produce a swoosh of arterial blood.

The hardest disposal of all was the emptied purse itself It went with her
everywhere and it showed in the wear and tear. The leather was

scarred and
softened and the stitching on the shoulder strap and where her hand would go in
and out had become frayed. It would sit beside her in the car; on the chair next to
her at restaurants; on her kitchen counter at home. I caressed it, memorizing its'
angles and planes and explored the worn pockets inside one last time where her
own fmgers had once been so many times.

When I went to the garbage can to throw it in I stood there for the longest time.
The lid in one hand, the purse poised over the opening, it felt like time froze.
Breath held, I couldn't move, nor could I release my grasp. In the end, with grief
stitched into my soul and pain soldered to my bones, I brought it back into the
house, like an orphaned child, and tucked it safely away in the back of my closet.

CATEGORY 2 FORMAL VERSE AWARD
(Shakespearean Sonnet)

JOYCE SHIVER
Crystal River, Florida

The Weeping Willow

We'd met beneath the tree for many years.
It sheltered us from rain or gave us shade.
It heard our secrets, shared our joys and tears,
and listened to the promises we made.
Through school and college, still our meeting place,
this leafy bower in the heart of town,
until that fateful day. I saw his face;
his walk was hesitant, he wore a frown.
He didn't want to hurt me, so ~e said,
but he had news that almost broke my heart.
He'd met another — they were soon to wed;
his vow of friendship just a stinging dart.
Now ten years later, back in town I see:
the willow tree still weeps; it weeps for me.

CATEGORY 3 LISTENING AWARD

BARBARA BLANKS
Garland, Texas

The Sounds of Summer

In the street of a Detroit neighborhood
we jumped rope
to the *swish swash swish swash* rhythm
of "Cinderella, dressed in yella,
went downstairs to kiss her fella-"

Thrown by bored boys,
the steady *pop swoosh* of tennis balls
against sun-glared brick walls
of The Parkside Projects
made hot-footed flies
buzz and land and *buzz.*

Up and down Stringham Court
baseball cards *clackety flap flap clackety flap*
between the spokes of my brother's bike wheels,
blending with the *rumble rumble whir*
of metal-wheeled roller skates
clamped tight to my sister's shoes.
My pogo stick and I thumped counterpoint
in *sproing swack sproing swack.*

Mostly I loved to *clomp clunk clomp*
on my wooden stilts-
taller than the other kids ...
at least for a little while.

CATEGORY 4 TOMOKA POETS AWARD (At the Beach)

PETER M. GORDON
Orlando, Florida

Sheltie

For centuries Shetland Islanders fed themselves
fishing rough Atlantic waters in *sixareens,*

sailing half a dozen men to the *haaf,* where Shetland's
island shelf drops to deep ocean, and fish swarm.

I think of those North Atlantic outposts while standing
on a Florida coast, thousands of miles and hundreds

of years from the home of my sheltie, Robbie's ancestors.
Robbie runs to the ocean's edge and races green waves

as they foam and scamper up sand to the tide line.
Shetland fishermen called themselves *haafmen,* created

a secret language to keep ocean spirits quiet even while
men floated above to steal sustenance from ocean depths.

Haafmen sailed without clock or compass, *sixareens* dancing
between swells and spray, finding their way home following

Moder Dy, the Mother Wave, to the mainland or outer islands
named *Unst, Yell,* and *Muckle Roe.* My dog is a Florida native.

He inherited his sharp bark from shelties who herded sheep
through roaring gales and waves when shelties had a job,

and a purpose. Today Robbie's bark serves only to warn salesmen
to approach our porch with caution and scare squirrels out of

our backyard. Sea birds hover head high, flapping wings
frantically to stay steady amidst wind gusts. Robbie circles

around my feet, barking, to corral gulls. What is my purpose?
Tides rise, and fall. Waves break. I feel sand shift under my feet.

CATEGORY 5 WILLARD B. FOSTER MEMORIAL AWARD
(Threat to the Environment)

B. ALEXANDER
Cambridge, Ontario, Canada

Let the Trees Breathe

Today, I am drawn in, past scrub spruce
scattered at the outermost edge,
through new growth, sprouting
like beard stubble on a flat face,
deeper into its clean scent,
further through the yellow swish of leaf molt,
and the softened purple of shadows.

Heritage skyscrapers, masters of our universe,
knife their way through the canopy,
light filtered in pale gold patches on the young,
as they study the handbook of survival,
set their roots, mold paths to sunlight,
hold this earth in tight embrace.

Genteel boughs brush my face:
I discover the password through
the invisible gate, <u>mn</u> transported
into the sacred heart of the forest,
permitted to press my face against
the toughened hide of mother trees
who recall tomahawks,
nibble of wood bison,
scent of longhouse fires,
as only moments past.

I stroke pulsing trunks, absorb their power,
listen to their heartbeats, understand
these guardians of our world, so important,
wish them dominance over land-grab barons.

JANET WATSON
Wesley Chapel, Florida

Your Disney World Credit Card

buys mouse ears of every color,
mouse ears of every size,
beaded, sequined, velveteened,
Mickey-Minnie merchandise,

Goofy sweatshirts, *Pluto* caps,
swirling *Princess* gowns,
Aladdin's magic carpet,"
Snow White's hand-me-downs,

Pooh Bear's sticky honeypot,
Storm Trooper figurines,
Moana's favorite surfboard,
Captain Nemo's submarine,

Frozen dolls and *Bambi* charms,
(one hundred dollars and up!),
Buzz Lightyear's nifty space ship,
a *Mary Poppins* travel cup,

Cinderella slippers,
Woody's cowboy hat,
Beauty and the Beast washcloths,
(if you can imagine that!).

The kids plead *Please?*
You're still accosted.
You're weak in the knees.
Your credit's exhausted.

Overwhelmed by the choices,
you now steer clear
of those dizzy shops
that sell Disney gear.

CATEGORY 7 JUNE OWENS MEMORIAL AWARD
(Secret Languages)

AMY WRAY IRISH
Lakewood, Colorado

Speaking Serpent

When I approach the shadows
she pauses her slim, slate form.

Doubles back and flickers the black fork
of her tongue to double check

If it's safe to talk. She cannot speak,
of course, but even in silence

Communicates much with the coil
and calligraphy of her body.

With mine, I move in supplication,
dance the words to my dangerous ask.

In response, she swims through the grass,
asking *Where?* and *When?*

With every curve. Scales a shimmer
of her Morse code message.

My hands flutter the answer: *Here*
and *Now.* At this she stiffens, darts swift

As an arrow. Points the way
to escape Eden.

And is forever branded
a dark serpent

Of questionable intent
rather than one sister

Showing another
how to shed her useless skin.

CATEGORY 8 THE POET'S VISION AWARD
(Any Form, Any Subject)

LLEWELLYN MCKERNAN
New Smyrna Beach, Florida

To The Carver From The Wood

Take me from the branch that tiptoes up,
the sap in my veins tingling at your touch.
Leave my shoulder blades their pale winged seeds.
Brush a bit of the earth on the soles of my feet.

Knob my knees. Bud my nose.
Swivel my neck, cut ten perfect toes.
Carve knuckles that knock, a head that bows.)
Make my arms and legs move, only you know how.

Cut me laughing eyes that ponder what's good
and open palms with rings of heartwood.
Purse my lips. Make them whistle.
Sew me a suit from weeds and thistle.

Carve my ears to open wide
so all that's sound goes deep inside.
Lathe my belly with a belt so tight
sawdust will be my deli-delight.

Sand what's rough to smooth satin skin.
Don't make it thick. Don't make it thin.
Polish my flesh till it gleams like the sun.
It will light up my world when the long night comes.

Pare my thoughts to the edge of a blink.
They'll feed the fire that burns when you think.
Put a priceless truth on the bark of my tongue,
so I'll have a treasure when everything's gone.

Whittle me short. Whittle me long.
Whittle me a fiddle to playa song
passionate and pure as a wild rose bloom.
Make it so lovely wooden hearts swoon.

CATEGORY 9 NEW RIVER POETS AWARD
(In Honor of Our Deceased Members)

NANCY SIMMONDS
Ft. Wayne, Indiana

Song of the Celestial Voyager

dawn unfolds over the cemetery
like the sweet voice of a single violin
beginning the concerto of the day
a pastel song etching the marble
tinting the frosted grass
accompanying a cantata of sparrows
hidden in the shadows of the trees
calming restless souls
and those who mourn

CATEGORY 10 VILLANELLE AWARD

VON S. BOURLAND
Happy, Texas

I Dream of an Eternal Garden

Azaleas shrub the garden of my dreams -
vie flames with brilliant fuchsia-tinted blooms
while off-white blossoms swirl like whipping cream

that glows while bathed in moonlight's beam.
With baby-pink and salmon-painted plumes
azaleas shrub the garden of my dreams.

They cling together like a quilters seam
or warp and weft crisscrossing weaver's loom
while off-white blossoms swirl like whipping cream

in mounds of fluffy petals - flowing streams -
a living banquet - pollen bees consume.
Azaleas shrub the garden of my dreams.

My stressful life at times bears silent screams.
The pain I hold inside produces gloom
yet off-white blossoms swirl like whipping cream

where heaven paints this vivid color scheme.
Lush promises of peace dispel my gloom.
Azaleas shrub the garden of my dreams
when off-white blossoms swirl like whipping cream.

CATEGORY 11 HUMOR AWARD

JOHN F. FOSTER
Sun City Center, Florida

A Light Touch

She chooses from her sexy lingerie
A filmy, lacy number just for him.
She slips it on, the essence of "risque",
And slides into their bed; the lights grow dim.

Her husband's hands explore beneath the sheets,
His palms descending with increasing verve.
She now begins to shiver as she greets
His glancing touch, exciting every nerve.

The softest moan beseeches from her lips
As searching fingers further down then drop
And brush along her tantalizing hips ....
He stops. She pleads, "Oh, honey, please don't stop!

> *Hey, why'd you quit?", her voice a puzzled note.*
> *His calm reply: "I found it .... the remote. "*

CATEGORY 12 THE LIVE POETS SOCIETY AWARD
(The Dark Side)

AMY WRAY IRISH
Lakewood, Colorado

What She Learned at School

Strangulation was the subject introduced
via cartoon. At lunch, my second-grade class
watched and laughed as a crooked, thorny weed
with villainous mustache sneered and crept
in exaggerated stance towards an unsuspecting

Girl-flower. The film delivered a clear visual
of her body swaying back, back, in his grip.
Her leafy fingers clawed at weed-thick hands
around her throat. The audio just as accurate:
a choking, wet gargle. Her whimper

When he squeezed. And he had a reason:
the girl's ear-piercing, nerve-grating,
blonde-petaled babble. She wouldn't stop.
So the cartoonist gave the weed leave
to stifle the sound. To shake her like a ragdoll.

When she finally quieted, the weed winked
at the audience. A job well done. He smirked
at her sheepish wilt, pathetic cough. Chuckled
as the carousing soundtrack played, spelling
out the lesson. And I learned who'd laugh along-
Everyone in the room but me.

CATEGORY 13 MIAMI POETS AWARD
(Trees)

BETTY ANN WHITNEY
Wesley Chapel, Florida

Life After Death

> *It is said that there is more life
> in a dead tree than a living one.*

Among the strangely beautiful
woodland trees, it is possible to forget
oneself in time and place ...

but today, a sudden rush of wind thrusts
in with hard driven rain, tearing through
leafy branches of grown trees, breaking
limbs, stripping bark, pulling and stretching
roots-uprooting a tree to fall, limb by limb
to the bare ground, to its eventual death.

Yet out of tragedy such as this, renewal
is given to the woods. Space for air
and light opens for the younger trees,
struggling in shadow.

In the deep oval holes of the fallen tree,
colonies of ants, birds, wasps and bees,
even raccoons, squirrels, rabbits, mice,
will come to settle into its warmth-
to live within its heart, for rest, for food,
for mating and nesting, as the tree
slowly erodes to earth.

CATEGORY 14 KATE KENNEDY MEMORIAL AWARD
(Any Form, Any Subject)

LAVERN SPENCER MCCARTHY
Blair, Oklahoma

Algebraic Angst

At first I thought I'd like that class a lot,
concerning math that I already knew.
An algebraic wizard I am not.

I solved for X and Y but soon forgot)
to square my eight with six and forty two.
At first I thought I'd like that class a lot.

Our demon teacher tested on the spot
with long equations I could never do.
An algebraic wizard I am not.

I did my work and whined. My grades were shot
because of knowledge I could not accrue.
At first I thought I'd like that class a lot.

I try my best at times but cannot blot
that subject. It has knocked my mind askew!
An algebraic wizard I am not.

Have pity, please, and do not ask me what
I learned in school. I haven't got a clue.
At first I thought I'd like that class a lot.
An algebraic wizard I am not.

CATEGORY 15 WEINBAUM/GLIDDEN AWARD
(Issues and Concerns Faced by LGBTQ Community)

PETER M. GORDON
Orlando, Florida

Dazzler

My neighbor Jane told me her son Alan was transitioning,
so I asked about his new job. She explained he injected
hormones weekly, dressed in high heels, short skirts, wigs,
full makeup, to prepare for his operation.

I played catch with Alan, coached little league after Jane's
husband left, and my first thought was how I failed him, not
providing a strong male role model. Jane said "they're home
now. Want to say hi?" and I asked if Alan had a boyfriend. Jane
said her son did not want to be called

"him" any more, since he was no longer a "he," and preferred
'they' for a pronoun. I thought how sad her son risked ridicule,
side effects, surgery, pain, to create this new self. Then I heard
high heels clicking on asphalt, lifted my head and saw
a knockout blonde woman walk down Jane's driveway.

She said "Hi" to me in a deep baritone, gracefully removed
letters from the mailbox, smiled, and walked back up toward the
house,

and I said, "was that . . . ?" and Jane said "Yes."
"They're beautiful," I said, and Jane said "Yes."

How dazzling when we show the world our true selves.

CATEGORY 16 HENRIETTA & MARK KROAH FOUNDERS
AWARD (Wedding)

DIANE NEFF
Longwood, Florida

Wedded

When I think back to signing forms to file
and pledging alii am and have to you,
our most important day was not on cue
from pastors, not from walking down the aisle
or capturing each moment with a smile.
We said the simple words, a soft [(I do"
not knowing how, but still creating new
our path to build our loving domicile.
The time I celebrate is not that day
but ordinary moments that we live -
the night you cradled our first child to sleep,
the note you penned with crayon just to say
"I'd do it all again," the hugs you give
are wedded to my heart, now yours to keep.

CATEGORY 17 PAST PRESIDENT'S AWARD
(Answers)

JUDI GERARD HOUGHTON
Middleburg, Florida

The Question

I was bound not by word to the man
Whose children I bore;
That ignoble title was held by another woman
Yet I pressed her skirts, bathed her mother.
And I grew to love her children as I did my own,
Forbidden though I was
To acknowledge their kinship.

It gave me odd -comfort to know
They loved me as well.
     For his wife knew all along of the terror)
He visited on me when I was but a girl myself
Perhaps she didn't actually hear me
Sobbing for my Papa as her husband
Half carried half dragged me
To the thatch of willows but, surely she heard,
As could the hands in the field,
My screams as he entered me.
Years later I would remember that I became
Quite solicitous of him,
Desperate not to repeat whatever I had done
To cause him such anger. It, of course, was not
Anger nor, was it to be an insular episode.

As I entered my teens and grew into a woman
I showed him even more consideration only
To bid his attention from our daughter.
I prayed every night God relieve me this burden
But, time would prove my only ally.
The long, long years eventually passed
Taking a greater toll on his mind than his body.
Once in a moment of queer tenderness he asked
Would I have given him my love freely.
How is a slave to know?

CATEGORY 18 FRANK YANNI AWARD
(Books)

TIM SCHULZ
Venice, Florida

The Lean-To circa 1969

A young boy toils at his chores
Such a daunting task indeed
Piles of refuse floor to ceiling
Within a box buried deep
Treasures disguised as trash
Classic examples of literature
The Works of Victor Hugo
included among the bounty
Bindings worn appearing as tattered
as the beggars of the Cour de Miracles
pillaging the streets of medieval Paris
Titles legible but just
Spines cracked, fragile
Inlays show, left as exposed as
the bosom of Zara, the bather
Hinges split barely attached
Front boards hang precariously like
Frollo from the heights of Notre Dame
before being cast down to his death
Leather moldy and rotting
Victimized by time and decay
Like the intertwined skeletons
of Quasimodo and Esmeralda
Pages yellowed, faded, brittle
Text archaic in style, yet
relevance fresh and insightful
Though the author's times have passed
Their messages endure timeless
Welcoming all that seek to be immersed
into the worlds betwixt the covers

CATEGORY 19 ANY SUBJECT
(Any Form, Any Subject)

LYNN SCHIFFHORST
Winter Park, Florida

Coming!

When I was ten,
I could touch the sky.

Why didn't I then
take down some stars
and keep them

to light up my pockets?

Instead the sky
took up some pieces of me
and kept them.

Now, night after night,
I hear myself call myself
among the stars.

And a voice from my pocket
cries, "Corning!"

Stan K. Sujka, Fishing Boat at Sunrise on Lake Virginia

FSPA STUDENT POETRY CONTEST
JUNIOR DIVISION

Brianna Decker

Callahan Middle School,
Teacher: Christina Cadigan
School District: Nassau

It's Made Me Depressed

If my world filled with silence,
I couldn't care less.
No more wailing sirens,
To fill me with stress.
The laughs of peers,
Fall on deaf ears,
Yelling and screaming,
Don't leave tears streaming.
Footsteps at night,
Won't fill me with fright.

If my vision waned,
I wouldn't be pained.
I'd not worry about my looks,
Or stare at textbooks.
Never again looking at a mirror,
or watching the judging jeerer,
But the faces of loved ones fade away,
No matter how much I beg them to stay.

After years and years,
Of not letting out tears,
Of keeping feelings suppressed,
Of words I haven't confessed,
Who would have guessed?
It's made me depressed.

Grade Six, 2nd Place

Lucas Cross

Callahan Middle School,
Teacher: Allison DeWitt
School District: Nassau

Basketball

Dribble, Dribble
that's the sound
of a basketball hitting the ground
right, left
5 seconds left
dribble, dribble
down the court
up. down
all around
take the shot
its getting hot
swish
that's the
sound of
a basketball
on it's
way to
the ground

Grade Six, 3rd Place

Ethan Waddell

Callahan Middle School
Teacher: Allison DeWitt
School District: Nassau

The world around you

The trees look bare
The temperature gets cooler
The snow falls from the sky
Just look at the world around you

New life is born
It feels warmer than normal
All the beautiful colors
Just look at the world around you

With the sun in the sky
The temperatures rise
Ice cream and water rides
Just look at the world around you

The leaves start to fall
All the colors change
Animals get ready for their long sleep
Just look at the world around you

SIXTH GRADE HONORABLE MENTION

1st HM: Mackenzy Wheeler
Title: A FRIEND
School: Callahan Middle School Nassau County
Teacher: Rebekah Mizenko

2nd HM: Jardin Cox
Title: HOME SICK
School: Callahan Middle School Nassau County
Teacher: Lauren Debolt

3rd HM: Kendyal Love
Title: MY GRANDPA
School: Callahan Middle School Nassau County
Teacher: Allison DeWitt

Grade Seven, 1st Place

Madilyn Hagney

Pine View School, Osprey, Florida
Teacher: Mrs. Cheryl Steele
Sarasota County Schools

The Eyes

I won't be able to sleep tonight
because they're still on me.
Those eyes.
Those pale eyes staring from my tv screen.
The pale eyes watching from the shadows.
Disembodied, sinister.
They send chills up my spine.
I can hear the breath from the mouth
that belongs with those eyes.
Measured, quiet
I can feel the phantom touch
of the hands that belong with those eyes
reaching out to me.
Cold, lifeless.
I can feel the being, the creature
with those pale, deep-set eyes
is lurking somewhere here.
Watching, waiting
to crawl from a vent
or drop from the ceiling.
I see them in every comer.
Every shadow.
Under every bed.
Even now I can feel their stare.
Some faceless, nameless entity
whose eyes bore into my very soul.
Unblinking, unwavering.
All I can see are the eyes.
Those eyes.

Grade Seven, 2nd Place

Jocelyn Eaton

Sebastian River Middle School
Teacher: Dr. Twila Patten
School District of Indian River County

Why

Days of darkness,
Days of sorrow,
This is a pill that's hard to swallow,
But it'll get better,
If you can just pull through,
Day by day,
But that's up to you.
No one can force you to get better,
No pill can force you to be happy,
If you can push yourself one day at a time,
That's enough to know,
You won't drop it on a dime.
Life is a gift,
A gift meant to be difficult,
A gift with obstacles,
A gift with a lesson,
That not everything will be handed over to you.
Not everything is perfect,
Not everything is brand new,
Your actions are chosen only by you.
You can get better,
But you have to try,
Nothing gets better when you just ask "Why?"

Grade Seven, 3rd Place

Michael Lopez

Fox Chapel Middle School
Teacher: Mrs. Karen Wright
School District: Hernando County

To My Mother

You never said I'm leaving,
You never said goodbye,
You were gone before I knew it,
And only God knew why.

Each morning when we awake,
We know that you are gone,
And no one knows the heartache,
As we try to carry on.

I remember everything about you,
Your voice, smile, beauty, and touch.
The way you walked,
The way you talked.

You are gone from me now,
But one thing they can't take away,
Your memory resides inside my heart,
And lights up my darkest days.

SEVENTH GRADE HONORABLE MENTION

1st HM: Devyn Quinn
Title: THE OCEAN BREEZE
School: Sebastian River Middle School Indian River County
Teacher: Dr. Twila Patten

2nd HM: Iveri Jefferson
Title: IT'LL BE A PERFECT 10
School: Sebastian River Middle School Indian River County
Teacher: Dr. Twila Patten

3rd HM: Abigail Hynes
Title: MARLEY
School: Challenger Middle School Lee County
Teacher: Amy Pontius

Grade Eight, 1st Place

Safire Holmes

Malone Middle School
Teacher: Brian Andrew Chalker
School District: Jackson

Monster

There is something,
that is inside me.
It's something I can't see,
with just the naked eye.

It may take a week or months,
to finally see,
the thing inside me.

The thing is taking over.
The air around me is becoming colder.
Every step I take,
every smile I fake,
it is showing,
the monster I am becoming.

Grade Eight, 2nd Place

Erin Bice

Challenger Middle School
Teacher: Mrs. Amy Pontius
Lee School District

I Miss You Everyday

They always say how hard it is to lose someone
I never quite understood
Just how deep it hurts knowing that death won.

I miss you everyday
No matter how much I cry
Or how much I pray
Or how high I know you fly
I still miss you every day.

The pain inside doesn't just unbind
Your laugh still stands out in my mind,
It's something I will never forget
I wish we spent more time together,
That's something I regret.

You introduced me to so much
F or that I could never repay
A thousand words can't bring you back
I miss you everyday.

You always talked about the arts,
It's something we hold dear to our hearts.

This poem is dedicated to you
Even though right now I am feeling blue.

We never made it to Broadway
But at least, for today,
Good-bye, I love you
And I miss you every day.

Grade Eight. 3rd Place
Joah Guerrero

Sebastian River Middle School
Teacher: Deborah Taflinger
Indian River County School District

The Wind

Over the land and seas
A hidden force
Moving cross the land and seas.
It carries many objects
like secrets and messages from distant land
it carries balance from light and dark
Over the land and seas
It brings peace to one and another.
It brings life from other distant areas
Life that can save more life
It moves other objects than life to help
But there is always balance.
Over the land and seas
It brings destruction
Moving life that destroys other life
Moving other objects than life that destroys life
Bring both at the same time
Over the land and seas
The force brings light and dark
Life and death
Balance
and this force is the wind

EIGHTH GRADE HONORABLE MENTION

1st HM: Jayden Calderon
Title: NFL
School: Sebastian Middle School Indian River County
Teacher: Deborah Taflinger

2nd HM: Cameron Joyner
Title: LOVE
School: Lavilla School of the Arts Duval County
Teacher: Nancy Lee Bethea

3rd HM: Candence Bertka
Title: A LETTER TO MY FUTURE SELF
School: Lavilla School of the Arts Duval County
Teacher: Nancy Lee Bethea

FSPA STUDENT POETRY CONTEST
SENIOR DIVISION

Grade: Nine, 1st Place

Monica Stevens

Flagler Palm Coast High School
Teacher: Shanna Graifer
Flagler County Schools

I've lived a thousand and one lives

I've lived a thousand and one lives,
each more different than the last.
I've lived a thousand and one lives,
felt pain, cried, and laughed.
I've lived a thousand and one lives,
drawn my last breath, seen the red sm rise.
I've lived a thousand and one lives,
held someone' s hand while they cried.
I've lived a thousand and one lives,
got my heart broken, fallen in love.
I've lived a thousand and one lives,
and was able to fly far above.
I've lived a thousand and one lives,
and made my share of mistakes.
I've lived a thousand and one lives,
Seen hot deserts, and snowflakes.
I've lived a thousand and one lives,
made of paper and ink.
And I shall never truly die,
because a piece of me exists
in every one of those book's lines.

Grade Nine, 2nd Place

Jaden Smith

Flagler Palm Coast High School
Teacher: Shanna Graifer
Flagler County Schools

Dorian

The wind blows, nights and days prior.
As it creeps closer, gust speeds rise higher.
While anxiety builds, one is deprived,
Of the rest, the rest. needed to thrive.

Televisions spread the news far and wide.
No place to run, no place to hide.
Days pass, like seconds on a clock.
The days, nearing, tick tock, tick tock.

Towns go vacant hours before.
Patterns of wood are mounted on doors.
Food supply depleted.
Water nonexistent.
Fuel tanks run dry.
Only one sound in the distance, a lone soul's cry.

The force is soon to arrive, yet questions remain.
Will they survive?
Will life be the same?

Trees are tossed around like paper bags.
Homes crumble like playing card towers.
Rain and floods saturate the land,
Disaster was inevitable, even if one planned.

Through the terror shines a single light.
It's the burning spirits of those hosting a fight.
Though the disaster was inevitable,
one thing would always stand:
No matter what, this was their homeland.

Grade Nine, 3rd Place

Zander Zaidel

Flagler Palm Coast High School
Teacher: Shanna Graifer
Flagler County Schools

Darkness

The air fills with black
Darkness engulfs the hot blue heavens
The noisy small town fades to silence
Children's fun and joy turns to stillness

The pale moon lights up the city
The bright, hot sun burrows away like a bear
Stars begin to appear like ants from the ground
Suspicion raises as the sky turns darker

The air fills with black
The population puts their drizzy head to rest
Adolescents dream of sweet dreams,
Some nightmares of horror

Some seek greatness, others strength
New days bring new opportunities, some gloom
People wake to families, others high paying jobs
Everyone has new beginnings, a new day brings it

The air fills with black
The moon begins to move further west,
The sun continues up from the east
When the sun rises, everyone awakes

When moon sets the dark goes away,
People wake to brightness and hope again
Then later on the darkness comes back,
And everything happens allover

NINTH GRADE HONORABLE MENTION

Erika Graham Sibley
Title: CRUSH
School: Matanzas High School Flagler County
Teacher: Shanna Graifer

Celeste Baker
Title: I AM WAR
School: Matanzas High School Flagler County
Teacher: Shanna Graifer

Alexis Rausch
Title: STARRY NIGHT
School: Matanzas High School Flagler County
Teacher: Shanna Graifer

Grades Ten and Eleven, 1st Place

Karis Knoll

New World School of the Arts
Teacher: Christian Losa
Miami-Dade Public School

I'm Afraid

The IV pumps a feeling of what should feel like good
I want to pump out the rest, leave my body to dust
Until there is nothing left but love's grasp
This isn't an obituary
T don't wish to die
But if! did, I don't want it to be in vain
my body strangles me in my veins
I take care of my heart, though I let it break
The storm, enough to wear down on the mask I wear
I only want it to end if I could call you my friend
And know someone would miss me
The very opportunity to sing this song to you so sweet
A song of remembrance, love, and bittersweet retreat
I wish the best for this fragile marble of a world
Though I don't plan on leaving it
But as I hit the pillow,
the succubus mask hits my eyes
This world is no longer mine
our hearts are no longer functioning as one
No more let's just hold on ... I'm off into space
A time that you can't embrace
My own little oasis,
With Its special snowflake taste
I awake and the flavor isn't one to savor
The stale tang of a twist into light
I'm glad to return though it feels like a bite
Nothing has changed through my body colonized by scopes
What is found in this body held together taped with wishes
I'm not afraid of dying—I'm afraid of not living

Grades Ten and Eleven, 2nd Place

Sofia Martinez

New World School of the Arts
Teacher: Christian Losa
Miami Dade County

Secrets of the Darkness

The sky unfolds, the darkness weeps
in all its mystery covered in stars and unspoken dreams.
The moon is silent, the earth is still,
all is hushed amid the clouds with their dew drops of arctic chill.
The silk wind, the silver breeze,
the music of the night whistling amongst the trees.
The tales of the untold, the stories that forebode
the secrets of the darkness that begin to unfold.
The glittering night sky, the abyss of endless tales,
secrets of prophets sung by acoustic nightingales.
The moon, the conductor of the symphony of the night,
orchestrating the harmonies that enchant the twilight.
The feeble stars, casting spells and constellations
alluring the chimes of the curious into dire temptation.
The night knows no danger, not to those who know,
the darkness is the enemy to those who fear the unknown.
The chamber of oceans, the crests of mountains,
each increment, a chronicle of years forgotten.
The void of caverns, the bellows of caves,
cries of nostalgia echo through acoustic alpha waves.
The shadows who lurk, figures rising from the stream,
fantasies of the darkness conquer those who dream.
The darkness is no foe though we have claimed it to be so
for it is the womb of sacred gems that glisten and glow.
The curtain draws, the stars take their final bow,
for all that once was is gone, there is only what is now.
The stars begin to fade, ascending further into the sky,
the darkness surrenders to the dawn of golden cry.

Grades Ten and Eleven, 3rd Place

Jackeline Petichakis

New World School of the Arts
Teacher: Christian Losa
Miami-Dade County

Delicate Ringing

A sound, a dream, a waltz, a scene, how clean.
The music box is working past a cry.
Its singing captivates. Its ring so keen
that no one mimicked. No one dared to try.

How precious, the music, like liquid gold.
The key. its servant, ever by its side.
But if the box grows old or green with mold,
attempting the key will prove it's dried.

You can surely get a small replacement
and fix it, quite as best as first received.
But even though the sound is heaven sent,
it will never, ever, be guaranteed.

My voice, as precious as a music box,
for if it break I'll sound like a yapping fox.

TENTH AND ELEVENTH GRADE
HONORABLE MENTION

1ST HM: Sofia Baraybar
Title: THE JOURNEY OF LOSING YOUR LOVED ONE
School: New World School of the Arts Miami Dade County
Teacher: Christian Losa

2ND HM: Sophia Camacho
Title: I CANNOT SLEEP
School: New World School of the Arts Miami Dade County
Teacher: Christian Losa

3RD HM: Nicole Anderson
Title: LITTLE THINGS
School: Spruce Creek High School Vol usia County
Teacher: Todd Palmer

Grade Twelve, 1st Place

Lindsey Collier

Spruce Creek High School
Teacher: Todd Palmer
Volusia County School District

Crescent Moon Smile

Your trailer sits in a meadow of dried yellow grass
Tucked miles away from the rest of the world.
The morning sun would shine through the window
As you softly shook me awake,
And greeted me 'good morning'
With that Crescent Moon Smile you always wore.

That day, you took my bike
And removed the training wheels.
Those big bodybuilder arms held me steady as I desperately
pedaled
Down the dusty gravel road.
Without those arms, I fell,
Bloodying my knees on sharp stones.
But you picked me up and washed my wounds
With that Crescent Moon Smile you always wore.

You started a bonfire that night
That glowed with the fire of the heavens.
We roasted marshmallows, side by side,
Because you knew that s'mores were my favorite.
Every marshmallow I touched burnt to black
No matter how hard I tried to fan the flames away.
So you handed me your own, toasted perfect golden brown,
With that Crescent Moon Smile you always wore.

But these are now memories, moments long gone.

Some night, when the rest of the world sleeps,
I'll drive back home
And bid that place a proper farewell.

And if I'm lucky, if the stars align,
You'll be there.
Arms wide open, waiting in the sky
With that Crescent Moon Smile you always wore.

Grade Twelve, 2nd Place

Jacob Wilhelm

Spruce Creek High School
Teacher: Todd Palmer
Volusia County School District

Our Place of Peace

Peace is a rare, intangible luxury,
Which we all seek to grasp with our hands.
Where the sun mirrors off amicable waters

Is where I pool together all my worries and anxieties
To pour them into the blue.
In return I am gifted with Peace.

Severe gusts recede to a gentle breeze.
Threat of thunderstorms dissolve into the water of tranquility.
Deafening whispers harmonize to the sweet, cordial chirps of
crickets
Singing in the mangroves.
Over the water I gaze over to waving dolphins,
Passing by in their pure state.
Stress of my toil evaporates into the savory saline air.

The agony fades away with the sun,
As the moonlight illuminates the nature around,
And radiates Peace upon me.
The undulating water beneath waves me a lullaby.
The darker it gets, the less there is to worry about.
Just me, the moon, and the soothing water.
Where nothing matters is our place of Peace.
We like it here.

Grade Twelve, 3rd Place

Serrie Gregor

Spruce Creek High School
Teacher: Todd Palmer
Volusia County School District

Emmeline

They say that when the Devil walks the earth
he does so with a slither

his forked tongue tastes bitter grit
while the cavernous pits upon his scaled face
pursue the scent of his next unfaithful victim
with no fear

your coiling around my hand tells me otherwise
you're terrified of heights, of my stepmother
and her loud shrieks
in open spaces as I encourage you to explore
you hide instead in my bag
as if you were pouting for me
to let you back into your safe cavern

my father explains to me about my stepmother,
that she believes God curses the sinful
to forever slither across the land
as you do
when I wriggle a writhing rat
your scaled nose pursuing
the scent of your weekly dinner

you are a dark omen,
and you are my light,
cursed as you are.

perhaps you're one of the lucky ones
who will have someone who loves you
forever and unconditionally

a platitude I struggle to believe
for myself

TWELFTH GRADE HONORABLE MENTION

1ST HM: Sofia Baraybar
Title: THE JOURNEY OF LOSING YOUR LOVED ONE
School: New World School of the Arts Miami Dade County
Teacher: Christian Losa

2ND HM: Sophia Camacho
Title: I CANNOT SLEEP
School: New World School of the Arts Miami Dade County
Teacher: Christian Losa

3RD HM: Nicole Anderson
Title: LITTLE THINGS
School: Spruce Creek High School Vol usia County
Teacher: Todd Palmer

About the Florida State Poets Association

2019-2020 FSPA OFFICERS

Al Rocheleau, President
Mary Marcelle, Vice-President
Leslie Halpern (deceased), Secretary
Robyn Weinbaum, Treasurer

2020-2021 FSPA OFFICERS

Mary Marcelle, President
Mark Andrew James Terry, Vice-President
Sonja Jean Craig, Secretary
Robyn Weinbaum, Treasurer

2019-2020 CERTIFIED FSPA CHAPTERS

Big Bend Poets, Tallahassee
Live Poets Society, Daytona Beach
Miami Poets, Pinecrest
New River Poets, Pasco County
North Florida Poetry Hub, Jacksonville
Orlando Area Poets, Maitland
Osceola Poetry Society, Osceola County
Poetry for the Love of It, Tallahassee
Space Coast Poets, Melbourne
Sunshine Poets, Crystal River
Tomoka Poets, Ormond Beach

FPSA also has many **members at large** who are not affiliated
with a chapter. These members live not only in Florida, but in
various states across the nation and countries around the globe.

NOTE: New members and chapters are welcome. Rules and
requirements are on the FSPA website:
www.floridastatepoetsassociation.org.

FLORIDA STATE POETS ASSOCIATION
History, Objectives, Conferences

The Florida State Poets Association Inc. was founded in 1974 by Henrietta A. Kroah of DeLand, Florida, with the assistance of Han Jurgenson, PhD, of the University of Tampa, a past president of the National Federation of State Poetry Societies (NFSPS). Its main objective is to secure a fuller public recognition of the art of poetry, stimulate a finer and more intelligent appreciation of poetry, and to provide opportunities for the study of poetry and incentives for the writing and reading of poetry. This is accomplished through local member chapters, a quarterly newsletter, and multiple state contests for adults and students. A State Convention is held each October and a spring-time conference is in April.

Visit: www.floridastatepoetsassociation.org
for current events, activities, and member news

* * *

NATIONAL FEDERATION OF
STATE POETRY SOCIETIES

NFSPS is a federation of over thirty state poetry societies. Organized in 1959 and incorporated in 1966, NFSPS provides support to the state member societies through a quarterly newsletter, various national contests, and a convention each June. Over the years FSPA members have been an integral part of the federation.

Visit: www.nfsps.com for further information